WELCOM
WITH WC

AN

MW00883405

Learning a new language can be both challenging and rewarding. This book provides puzzle based vocabulary exercises and is intended to supplement traditional methods of language study. We believe that learning should be fun. If you are doing something that you enjoy, then it will be easy to stick with.

In Learn ROMANIAN with Word Search Puzzles you will find a collection of 130 bilingual word search puzzles that will challenge you with dozens of interesting categories.

This book includes:
• Diverse categories including: Numbers, Colors, The Body, Weather, Professions, Fruits, Vegetables, Verbs, Opposites, and many more!
• Words hidden horizontally, vertically or diagonally in each puzzle
• Easy to read puzzles
• Challenging and fun!
• Puzzle based learning provides unique learning perspective
• 65 jumbled review puzzles to challenge your memory and lock in those translations with reinforcement learning
• Complete solutions provided.

Keep your Mind Active and Engaged
Studies have shown that continuously challenging your brain with puzzles and games or acquiring new skills such as a new language can help to delay symptoms of dementia and Alzheimer's.
Keeping a sharp mind is a great idea for people of any age.

Learn with Word Search Series
Revised and updated for 2018.
Now including 10 challenging languages. Check out our other titles!

Happy searching!

Te Iubesc!
Daniela.

To those who occasionally struggle to find the correct words.

Welcome to Learn with Word Search. It's time to count down to your new vocabulary. Here we go. Three. Two. One   Find these number translations in the grid below.

```
E R A W D O C B A X W T L B Ş D
C E C E Z E R P S I O D W O Ş O
E C X L Ş A C M T D O P E G A L
Z E N E V E S H F H A D T S P D
E Z I V E Q I N L O P Ş Ş Ş A S
R E F E N R S G T P U N S A I Ş
P R O N T O T L H A E R P P S R
S P K E V L E W T T Ă Ă T T P E
I S E L Ş B N Ş B R C N U E R N
E N T A O N W Ş Ă U O N T R E I
R U O E T E T I O A U W I E Z N
T A C S A E T V E E R H T H E P
L C I T E F F L S S A F E H C G
A X N Ş H T O I Ş H I O O A E F
H E C E Z Ă D U V F N W D Ă Ş G
J C I N C I S P R E Z E C E Ă I
```

ONE	UNU
TWO	DOI
THREE	TREI
FOUR	PATRU
FIVE	CINCI
SIX	ŞASE
SEVEN	ŞAPTE
EIGHT	OPT
NINE	NOUĂ
TEN	ZECE
ELEVEN	UNSPREZECE
TWELVE	DOISPREZECE
THIRTEEN	TREISPREZECE
FOURTEEN	PAISPREZECE
FIFTEEN	CINCISPREZECE

A zillion is often used to describe a huge number, but it doesn't actually have a defined value. We won't make you count to a zillion, but below you will find some more numbers to add to your vocabulary.

```
L N Ş S Ş T Y Ş A P T E Z E C I
I K O B I O P T S P R E Z E C E
L Ă N U Ş X D Ş N Ş W S I E Ş R
E Ş O Y Ă F T N N E E T Z Ă A I
Ă Y I T Ş Z O E A O W I L E P Ş
D T L H Ă I E R E S C T M V T A
E X L G L K Z C T N U S D O E I
R I I I A M I I I Y E O T P S S
D S M E F E C C O V Ş S H A P P
N N N I N E T E E N Ş U I T R R
U O F A Z H E N S Z E T R R E E
H T O Ă O P T Z E C I Ă T U Z Z
Y I U B S E V E N T Y A Y Z E E
E O T R E I Z E C I Ş T Ş E C C
D G T N O U Ă S P R E Z E C E E
E N Y T E N I N E E T H G I E A
```

SIXTEEN	ŞAISPREZECE
SEVENTEEN	ŞAPTESPREZECE
EIGHTEEN	OPTSPREZECE
NINETEEN	NOUĂSPREZECE
TWENTY	DOUĂZECI
THIRTY	TREIZECI
FORTY	PATRUZECI
FIFTY	CINCIZECI
SIXTY	ŞAIZECI
SEVENTY	ŞAPTEZECI
EIGHTY	OPTZECI
NINETY	NOUĂZECI
HUNDRED	O SUTĂ
THOUSAND	O MIE
MILLION	UN MILION

The seven days of the week were named after
the seven celestial bodies that were visible
to the naked eye thousands of years ago.
These are the Sun, Moon, Mercury, Venus, Mars,
Jupiter, and Saturn. See if you can spot
their translations with your naked eye below.

```
Y A P O Y E N Â B S I O O H M O
A O V M A M S T O O S U Ţ A E Â
S Ş Y A D O T Ă E G Â V H E S F
T Ă Y A D N U S P D M H J L F E
Ă T U E S D A Y S T B A U I Â R
Z C O N A A I Y Y P Ă E R W R Y
I Y I M J Y A A T M T M E Ţ Ş A
R A O N O D D N I R Ă E Â M I D
A D C I I R P E T R K Â Ş N T S
D R R R U M R H A E E R E H Ă E
G E F T Â C U O N Ş H N A Y Ă N
I T A W U R A D W F I I I E Â D
W S N R S C C E A Â N Z G V Ă E
A E I D Q T D T M U C M K E E W
T Y A D I L O H L A N O I T A N
Ă Y H E S Ă R B Ă T O A R E Ţ Ă
```

MONDAY	LUNI
TUESDAY	MARŢI
WEDNESDAY	MIERCURI
THURSDAY	JOI
FRIDAY	VINERI
SATURDAY	SÂMBĂTĂ
SUNDAY	DUMINICĂ
WEEKEND	SFÂRŞIT de săptămână
NATIONAL HOLIDAY	SĂRBĂTOARE naţională
TODAY	ASTĂZI
TOMORROW	MÂINE
YESTERDAY	IERI
WEEK	SĂPTĂMÂNĂ
DAY	ZI

The Roman calendar originally had ten months, which explains why September, October, November and December are based on the latin words for seven, eight, nine and ten. Search for the months and their translations below.

```
N R Ă W R X E E O N C R Y E A R
T S U G U A B W O J E A L H E E
E E N G Y N D I U B H D T B L B
A P R I L I E N O H E N M E N M
F S F D E M E T E I P E Ă I E E
S E G N B N C M O L C L E R F T
O P B R E O A C E E A A X A V P
R T I R M I T I D O I C E U E E
B E K D U O R E B M E V O N N S
A M O A M A Y B Y I Z I R A F O
U B A B U E R D M A Y R L I O V
D R R R A G A Y Ă E J D I U D E
S I B M C L U P T L C U L P I E
E E S A U H N S R U N E L N H H
F H T N O M A R T I E E D Y X V
E T Ă T S G J R E N L Y K R Ă I
```

JANUARY	IANUARIE
FEBRUARY	FEBRUARIE
MARCH	MARTIE
APRIL	APRILIE
MAY	MAI
JUNE	IUNIE
JULY	IULIE
AUGUST	AUGUST
SEPTEMBER	SEPTEMBRIE
OCTOBER	OCTOMBRIE
NOVEMBER	NOIEMBRIE
DECEMBER	DECEMBRIE
CALENDAR	CALENDAR
MONTH	LUNĂ
YEAR	AN

The seasons are caused by the tilt of the
Earth as it orbits the sun. For part of the
year the sun shines longer on one hemisphere
resulting in summer. Tilt your head and
search for these words related to time and the
seasons below.

```
N R L A H D H T N O M R H G H D
Y L V A R Ă Z A I M A Ă P U D Ţ
A E E G N I R P S T U N I M Ă D
Ţ L Y T Q M N A A N S T M N I J
N I R N H T O Y V E D U U N A G
Ţ E N E E I W R C Ă I L M A F O
O Ţ Z T F B I U N R M Y U M T I
I N O I E Z N T L I I I G R E A
E F E N S D T N P S N D R E R R
R I Ă H Ă J E E A E E G A P N N
Ţ A N Y E A R C C C A T A Y O Ă
Ă Y M I N U T E A O Ţ H P C O H
U R A P T Y D D S N Ă G O A N S
W L O C E S E B Ţ D S I A U O O
E Ţ T Ţ R L O N A O F N A I R N
F R G T R E O K V A N O T R R H
```

WINTER	IARNĂ
SPRING	PRIMĂVARĂ
SUMMER	VARĂ
AUTUMN	TOAMNĂ
SECOND	SECUNDĂ
MINUTE	MINUT
HOUR	ORĂ
DAY	ZI
MONTH	LUNĂ
YEAR	AN
MORNING	DIMINEAŢĂ
AFTERNOON	DUPĂ-AMIAZĂ
NIGHT	NOAPTE
DECADE	DECENIU
CENTURY	SECOL

COLORS

The three primary colors are red, green and
blue. These three colors can be combined to
create an astonishing variety of color.
Astonish yourself by finding these
translations in the grid below.

```
A K E D I A S C G E G S I T Ş S
D T Ş W D T N S N E I R R S H D
Ş H E R G T T N S A T E I O N E
S J U R G Ş D E S M D E E T Ş I
E A I C S A A I O Q T E R K O U
M A R O B F L O T N D N R R L R
I N U L Y V I B E R L D O A O T
Z E A N E E R G E F D T Z Ş S S
Y C T R A A R V C N N A S B D A
K E E Ş G U O G L P Ş D N Ş R B
T G L P F I D T H A K E A D D L
K N O L U L N W O R B L A C D A
N A I S O R E T I H W B H U R A
I R V G E W P C I L L O N O E H
P O R T O C A L I U O O T V D I
N M T T C T E S E H S Ş I O W L
```

BLACK	NEGRU
BLUE	ALBASTRU
BROWN	MARO
GOLD	AURIU
GREY	GRI
GREEN	VERDE
ORANGE	PORTOCALIU
PINK	ROZ
PURPLE	VIOLET
RED	ROŞU
SILVER	ARGINTIU
WHITE	ALB
YELLOW	GALBEN

A dodecagon has 12 sides, while a megagon has a million sides, at which point it is essentially a circle. Time to think outside the box and find these 2D and 3D shapes in the puzzle below.

```
A P O R E C T A N G L E B S Ă E
O E Ă N E S S O D D R Ă L J S H
D N E R E T G D I A M A N T E Ă
F T C E E A Y A U O N R N A H Ă
A A P T X F M Q N W R E O R R W
C G N E Ă O S O S O D E G T T Ă
U O H A N D C D T V C Ă A Ă A Z
B N H D S T I S E A B E X P W D
E L A V O M A M A L U E E N C F
V N P G A O T G A N C L H L N N
G E O R A T S L O R G R B E F O
G N Y C N V U R D N I L I C I G
S P H E R E W L A E R P W C W A
S S L S F E C I Ă N E X A J Y T
I H G N U I R T R E D N I L Y C
I H G N U T P E R D E I D L W O
```

CIRCLE	CERC
CONE	CON
CUBE	CUB
CYLINDER	CILINDRU
DIAMOND	DIAMANT
HEXAGON	HEXAGON
OCTAGON	OCTOGON
OVAL	OVAL
PENTAGON	PENTAGON
PYRAMID	PIRAMIDĂ
RECTANGLE	DREPTUNGHI
SPHERE	SFERĂ
SQUARE	PĂTRAT
STAR	STEA
TRIANGLE	TRIUNGHI

THE HEAD

Our face is the most expressive part of our body. We can convey a variety of emotions with the 43 muscles we have in our face.
Below are some words related to your face and head.

```
S Â D E E N E C N Â R P S I Y D
Ă L Y A T S D A E H E R O F Â G
M E H R E N O Z I I U I S A X J
R Y M R E H U N B Ţ G A A Ţ S Â
E E I N T N R R N T N H Â Ă D I
V B I I H A Ă Ă F V O I O D B Q
B R A H A B G P I T T L D T G A
P O T A R I Q Y A P U F Z D B W
E W B U G I U A I C C W M W T R
E S G R H E T H E U U S D E L H
G T Ă Ă A Ă N O R Ă L P E O Q H
Ţ H Ţ T U Z C E E R B U Z E H Â
R Y I D L H C H T U O M Ţ D E T
H T V L I H E Â E G W N I H C Z
O T E Y E L A S H E S P I L A H
P R F R I G N S M L K Â L E F O
```

CHEEK	OBRAZ
CHIN	BĂRBIE
EAR	URECHE
EYE	OCHI
EYEBROWS	SPRÂNCENE
EYELASHES	GENE
FACE	FAŢĂ
FOREHEAD	FRUNTE
HAIR	PĂR
HEAD	CAP
LIPS	BUZE
MOUTH	GURĂ
NOSE	NAS
TEETH	DINŢI
TONGUE	LIMBĂ

The human body is a remarkable thing, with hundreds of specialized parts that we take for granted every day. Here is a list of some important parts of the body to remember.

```
V A Â R E Ă F E Ş O L D Â N E N
O A Ă R U T E I E H C N Î R D Ă
U H Ă Î S E N H N L A A I Â Y E
O M S I A I T E T G B H I P S R
U O A T Ţ P V O D N E O M C H A
A W T A R S P I C I O R W R O M
T X Z Ţ N I Ă Ş I Ţ A R B Â U L
N S Ă S M Â G B Â R I Î I F L U
Ş P N F S F I F O S F Y R S D T
N O Â E O W G I T C T E Ă H E E
E E M M W T C L Ă I B E N O R G
N L A O O I E T E G M P B U B E
E Î P O P G A G C C U T Ă L L D
T T F P E L Ă Â E E H O T D A R
R O I C I P A L E D T E G E D C
Ă H H E D N V T B V H P Y R E U
```

ARM	BRAŢ
ELBOW	COT
FINGER	DEGET
FOOT	PICIOR
HAND	MÂNĂ
HIP	ŞOLD
LEG	PICIOR
NIPPLE	SFÂRC
SHOULDER	UMĂR
SHOULDER BLADE	OMOPLAT
THUMB	DEGETUL MARE
TOE	DEGET DE LA PICIOR
WAIST	TALIE
WRIST	ÎNCHEIETURĂ

THE BODY 2

Skin is the largest human organ and is approximately 15% of your body weight. Search for these other parts of the body and their translations in the puzzle grid below.

```
E E S D I A T N M S D Q J H K Ă
X N Ț H O I E N A W O S B O H A
L I R L F O H Â E H V N H R D E
I T S D O Y Ă E X Ă A I I S Z V
A H R S B H L Ț A A R T K S F L
N R T H Ă E T P I Â Y I I L A Â
R O M S I R Ț D S D N H A S C H
E A A P T G Ă E O Ă T C E I Ă Ț
G T S P I Â S B Ț S Â N R M A F
N Â H A Ț T P K M P B U O R O E
I S T I Ț B C R C A B N B A E S
F D L M G E A S O O G E O E I E
A E S E N H O C Ă C T G W R H T
R S E R V O E L K N A T I O G A
D N C F T A T S A E R B U F N P
K E G L E Z N Ă R A O U S B U S
```

ANKLE	GLEZNĂ
ARMPIT	SUBSUOARĂ
BACK	SPATE
BODY	CORP
BREAST	SÂN
BUTTOCKS	FESE
CALF	GAMBĂ
FINGERNAIL	UNGHIE
FOREARM	ANTEBRAȚ
KNEE	GENUNCHI
NAVEL	BURIC
NECK	GÂT
SKIN	PIELE
THIGH	COAPSĂ
THROAT	GÂT

ON THE INSIDE

Our internal organs regulate the body's critical systems, providing us with oxygen and energy, and filtering out toxins. Check out this list of squishy but important body parts.

```
M T S M A L L I N T E S T I N E
T U S K S T O M A C U E I Ă H A
E L S E I S T C I B E I S S E I
L A M C P D I D Ţ Ș N R A R A R
X R P L L F N I G Â K E E D R G
I G E H E E R E M N R T R H T G
D E D S P E S Ă Y C R R C G Y S
N I I A C E L D N A N A N F R Ș
E N H P R P S A O I M O A A V V
P T E C E N P T I O L E P B N E
P E C N I A R B T K L P O Ă T G
A S E E E N E S A Y N B S M S N
S T V R R V I F S L U S Ș I P Â
O I H C Ș U M R E V I L U N G S
H N Ţ Ţ W B O Ș A C W O S I N D
T E S O R G L U N I T S E T N I
```

APPENDIX	APENDICE
ARTERIES	ARTERE
BLOOD	SÂNGE
BRAIN	CREIER
HEART	INIMĂ
KIDNEY	RINICHI
LARGE INTESTINE	INTESTINUL GROS
LIVER	FICAT
LUNGS	PLĂMÂNII
MUSCLES	MUȘCHI
PANCREAS	PANCREAS
SMALL INTESTINE	intestinul SUBȚIRE
SPLEEN	SPLINĂ
STOMACH	STOMAC
VEINS	VENE

The Earth is an enormous place that time has divided up into continents and oceans. Take some time and memorize these words that define our Earth.

```
N O N I N O R T H P O L E H E T
D R O N E D A O C E A N U L C Y
V W A E C P A O P T A F R I C A
V N T T O O N C I O A S F J C L
L E A R L T N T I C L I I I T A
O O U E I A U T I T C U R A C T
N E N N C D N T I A C E L I A I
G D E G I O C T P N M R R S T T
I N R N I R C L I A E E A E U U
T E E O A T U I H C M N C T T D
U Q P T N N U T F A O U T A N E
D U N O A L R D H I A C I R F A
E A I E R O U T I T C S E E N V
S T C E N U U L O N A A H A A T
U O A I R O E R O T E T P C N E
D R U H S O U T H P O L E O I A
```

AFRICA	AFRICA
ANTARCTICA	ANTARCTICA
ASIA	ASIA
ATLANTIC OCEAN	OCEANUL atlantic
CONTINENT	CONTINENT
EQUATOR	ECUATOR
EUROPE	EUROPA
LATITUDE	LATITUDINE
LONGITUDE	LONGITUDINE
NORTH AMERICA	america DE NORD
NORTH POLE	POLUL NORD
PACIFIC OCEAN	OCEANUL PACIFIC
SOUTH AMERICA	america DE SUD
SOUTH POLE	POLUL SUD

Time to zoom in and take a look at some geographical features that make up our planet. Fly over mountains, forests and glaciers as you reflect on the beauty of nature.

```
Q E T A E T X S T H C A E B C C
C M R E C I F D E C O R A L I O
R U E F O R E S T A H I A D B R
E N Ş Â Â S I S R L Ş C H T H A
R T E U E T E N A E C O N B E L
U E D R F T B Ă S G L A C I E R
D Ţ T G F A R U Y U C S E Ş K E
Ă E Ş A O W O T Â L L T E S A E
P J G M R G I A U V C Ă I Ş L F
W Ş A S A C H V O O P R B C S S
O E Â L Ş R S E A L O D L L Ă S
T T T L P E E S Ţ C N E Ă Â Ş Ţ
Ş V A O O Ă T D E A V Ă O T L E
A O U T W F Ş A L N R V Ş D O Ş
R L R Â E H N S M O U N T A I N
O B C R E V I R T H G F D T A X
```

BEACH	PLAJĂ
CITY	ORAŞ
COAST	COASTĂ
CORAL REEF	RECIF DE CORALI
CRATER	CRATER
DESERT	DEŞERT
FOREST	PĂDURE
GLACIER	GHEŢAR
ISLAND	INSULĂ
LAKE	LAC
MOUNTAIN	MUNTE
OCEAN	OCEAN
RIVER	RÂU
SEA	MARE
VOLCANO	VULCAN

Today's weather forecast shows a 100% chance of learning some important weather terms.

```
F I E D S Z T E U B S D Z C C E
R K E N E K O T T D N M I B L W
B T I N N T C Ă D D R T E M O F
S I R O A T A Ă D A P Ă Z B U L
D E A D H T F E W T E T N L D H
N P I A B H E D O N H I G L Y E
S Y M Î E E E H U R A U A H R N
L D N T R M F I E R B I N T E A
U T D N U V S C Ă E O E N D T C
R F O R U E E D Ţ G I A O L E I
O U T R R S B C A L D A R O N R
Q Ţ I P A W H U E U G U O C U R
U Ţ F O G I S E C F A S S L T U
Ă A E O A U N T I R O S N Î P H
R G N I N T H G I L U A H O E E
C I R T E M O R A B F C M R W H
```

BAROMETRIC pressure	PRESIUNE barometrică
CLOUDY	NOROS
COLD	RECE
FOG	CEAŢĂ
HOT	FIERBINTE
HUMID	UMED
HURRICANE	URAGAN
LIGHTNING	FULGER
RAIN	PLOAIE
RAINBOW	CURCUBEU
SNOW	ZĂPADĂ
SUNNY	ÎNSORIT
THUNDER	TUNET
WARM	CALD

Let's go on a word safari to search for some of Africa's most famous animals. Elephants and lions are hiding somewhere below.

```
A T I A H I R C D R A P E H G Z
O S T D R A P O E L E Ă F I T D
N R I N O C E R E O L C F Q S A
N O O B A B G O R I L L A O U I
E I I O Ţ H P W R F T N R A M V
C A U L H A P O N N T E I H A A
H A B B R I G E A E C O G C T R
I N D D A E P F L O E I M I O Z
M E E A N B E O N E R S C R P E
P Y S W H L P I P A I S Ţ T O B
A H A T E E H C F O T R E S P R
N W R R R R I Ă A N T I L O P Ă
Z H B G L U N U E Z N A P M I C
E J E U O E Ţ Y E O O N M E H O
E O Z T I O T D Ţ L T V O Z R N
E T L H U A W Y E B A N I Ţ Ţ D
```

ANTELOPE	ANTILOPĂ
BABOON	BABUIN
CHEETAH	GHEPARD
CHIMPANZEE	CIMPANZEU
ELEPHANT	ELEFANT
GIRAFFE	GIRAFĂ
GORILLA	GORILĂ
HIPPOPOTAMUS	HIPOPOTAM
HYENA	HIENĂ
LEOPARD	LEOPARD
LION	LEU
OSTRICH	STRUŢ
RHINOCEROS	RINOCER
ZEBRA	ZEBRĂ

ANIMAL KINGDOM 1

A recent study estimated that there are approximately 8.7 million different species of life on Earth. Below are just a few examples for you to learn.

```
I V O Â G M S I O O R A G N A K
D R H Ă T T U R S P O L A R E D
Y X Ş U Â T R A T S E Ă E E E T
Ş E W T R C T B E X S N J M D F
I I R O H G H B H H R I N A A O
V S O B R D I I E A D M Ş H A C
H E N R Â E A T V R I U E Ş L R
K E Z I T S G L C U U R I H T N
T S A F A Ă I I E Ă L G A Ă A G
H U L O C D N L T A M P N L U P
R O I J C D I I J M Ă I E A B D
W M Ş A O E U A M C U N L A C Ş
T O T G P E G C I G I I U Ă H T
F O X U B U N S N Â Y T M H O W
S S R A A E I E C E R A O Ş E Q
D E N R T P P O L A R B E A R B
```

BAT	LILIAC
CAMEL	CĂMILĂ
CAT	PISICĂ
DOG	CÂINE
FOX	VULPE
JAGUAR	JAGUAR
KANGAROO	CANGUR
MOOSE	ELAN
MOUSE	ŞOARECE
MULE	CATÂR
PENGUIN	PINGUIN
POLAR BEAR	URS POLAR
RABBIT	IEPURE
TIGER	TIGRU
WOLF	LUP

Another study estimates that approximatley 150-200 species are going extinct every 24 hours. Find the animals below before they disappear forever.

```
E C O N O E E L I D O C O R C M
E E S H Ş L I D O C O R C T A S
Ş O Ş S N A T U G N A R U O S T
G G A F R O G H L N H Ă M G T M
M B R O A S C Ă G Z N U G R O T
S L P B T S Q U I R R E L R R R
O A E Q O B T N E S A M A L L Ă
N C I T N A B N N K N C A E A Ş
I K V R N E I E N A E A C O M R
P B E M A P G U B T L H K O Ă D
S E V V U R K U O Ş O O K E O S
C A E C U S F K O Ţ P A B W O N
R R R V N N S C N O C S L O S A
O O I Ţ I K T O S Ţ M L U L Ş S
P N Ţ Ţ A I O U P R E J I Ş Q D
L D Ă R F T M N E O S E L H E W
```

BEAVER	CASTOR
BLACK BEAR	URS NEGRU
CROCODILE	CROCODIL
FROG	BROASCĂ
LLAMA	LAMĂ
OPOSSUM	OPOSUM
ORANGUTAN	URANGUTAN
OWL	BUFNIŢĂ
PORCUPINE	PORC SPINOS
RACCOON	RATON
RAT	ŞOBOLAN
SKUNK	SCONCS
SNAKE	ŞARPE
SQUIRREL	VEVERIŢĂ

SEA LIFE

The blue whale is the largest animal on Earth. It's heart is the size of a car and can weigh as much as 50 elephants.   Search the depths of the puzzle below for some other fascinating sea creatures.

```
E D L S H S I F Y L L E J D E E
A S A O T S E T A C S A O R B R
T H L L U A E R A M A L A C A A
L A E L R C R A B E P H R M C M
I R W A T E S F L H S E O E A E
Q K A L L M E G I I T H L T R D
R F L N E Ț A N F S O A S A A A
K I R Ă N E L A B M H N M E C E
C S U P O T C O R W E E A A A T
C Ă S R O M L H G C D D I J T S
S J C Q C E H Z R U N E U T I E
T A A R U E S A E Ş F H L Z Ț Ş
G A I T O I B L C T Ă C O F Ă N
N V A D G Ă D G H N Ş A Ț C I R
S O W D E D S W I L H E R I W N
O E R B S T F E N A O O P I E D
```

TURTLE	BROASCA TESTOASA
CRAB	CRAB
DOLPHIN	DELFIN
FISH	PEŞTE
JELLYFISH	MEDUZĂ
LOBSTER	HOMAR
OCTOPUS	CARACATIŢĂ
ORCA	ORCĂ
SEA LION	LEU DE MARE
SEAL	FOCĂ
SHARK	RECHIN
SQUID	CALAMAR
STARFISH	STEA DE MARE
WALRUS	MORSĂ
WHALE	BALENĂ

Are you married? Do you have any siblings? Here is a list of terms that will help you to describe your nearest and dearest

```
O R F R E H T A F D N A R G P A
D R Ţ Ţ D S O M O T H E R Ţ R R
A S A N Ş M Ă E N T H V T T E M
U R F R A T E T E T H L E T H Y
G Y A M U I E U A S G Ă S R T O
H T Ă Ş Ş W N F Q R T I Ş O O Ş
T R Ă A X C E R A A S N P A M S
E D E C H L A H T Z S E E S D O
R F I I C Ă Ş A P O N Z I R N N
Ţ I I N B Ţ T T R E N O L I A E
Ş Ţ U U R U P Ă R I N Ţ I T R P
Ţ C E B O E N L Ă Z I F M U G O
I U C Z T O A I Y L I M A F F A
H A E E H D T E C I P D F U B T
P Ă I Q E N L T I Ă O X W S N Ă
C P N E R D L I H C C W W E N T
```

AUNT	MĂTUŞĂ
BROTHER	FRATE
CHILDREN	COPII
DAUGHTER	FIICĂ
FAMILY	FAMILIE
FATHER	TATĂ
GRANDFATHER	BUNIC
GRANDMOTHER	BUNICĂ
MOTHER	MAMĂ
NEPHEW	NEPOT
NIECE	NEPOATĂ
PARENTS	PĂRINŢI
SISTER	SORĂ
SON	FIU
UNCLE	UNCHI

FAMILY 2

Here are some more family members that you might be particularly fond of (or perhaps not)

```
L V W A L N I R E T H G U A D J
G O N Ă T S O N I N L A W N C D
R W T W E Ț O S N E O Ș A E E D
A A A A S L E O D O S B Y P E Ș
N L E L N O K A E N S R I O N G
D N G N N M C T H U A T A A R D
D I A I S I U R H V S R U T L V
A R B R N Ț R C E C B F G Ă E E
U E O E Y E T E Ă D I Ă Ă R Y Ă
G H Y T B D R N H R E F I W T E
H T T S A E E E O T C Ș F A I L
T A E I B P L C W O O Ă N Ț T H
E F A S O C R U U R T M O Ș A T
R N E T O H H S Ș Ă U S R S A O
N A Ă Ș E G I R L C X O Ă F M E
R C W A L N I R E H T O R B S S
```

BROTHER-IN-LAW	CUMNAT
BABY	BEBELUȘ
BOY	BĂIAT
COUSIN	VERIȘOR
DAUGHTER-IN-LAW	NORĂ
FATHER-IN-LAW	SOCRU
GIRL	FATĂ
GRANDDAUGHTER	NEPOATĂ
GRANDSON	NEPOT
HUSBAND	SOȚ
MOTHER-IN-LAW	SOACRĂ
SISTER-IN-LAW	CUMNATĂ
SON-IN-LAW	GINERE
WIFE	SOȚIE

Actions speak louder than words. Here is a list of common verbs that you might encounter in your travels.

```
E D F S T W O L L O F O T T O I
L J I Y A V A I N E N O O O G W
Ş Ş I V Ş Ş T A E O T H C S B E
A T S O R Ă H C A H E E O I T E
B Î Q L G H J Â I A A P O N I N
M Â E A A G X N R R D T K G Z T
I H L U V U K T E I A O O A U T
H Î T H E A N A T T G D R P A T
C Â M G D E M O T Ă Â H C M A M
S E P D E R S R O L N A A A I Y
A Y A E A E L Î U P D C Ş Î E E
A I T M E E T O W A I T K N Ş S
R A D V Â L R H Ă T E S G R T O
Ă R I Â B N S O I P A S N T E D
C F Y R R A C O T O E T S G Y R
A Î N T R E B A T O C H A N G E
```

TO ASK	A ÎNTREBA
TO BE	A FI
TO CARRY	A CĂRA
TO CHANGE	A SCHIMBA
TO COOK	A GĂTI
TO EAT	A MÂNCA
TO FOLLOW	A URMA
TO HEAR	A AUZI
TO PAY	A PLĂTI
TO READ	A CITI
TO SEE	A VEDEA
TO SING	A CÂNTA
TO SLEEP	A DORMI
TO THINK	A GÂNDI
TO WAIT	A AŞTEPTA

There are thousands of verbs in use today.
Here are some more popular verbs to practice.
Find the translations below.

```
S  M  I  Z  Ţ  R  A  S  E  L  Q  G  A  Y  S  A
A  C  Ă  L  Ă  T  O  R  I  Î  Î  E  L  E  H  W
V  K  N  I  R  D  O  T  A  W  T  R  C  Y  O  E
E  M  I  A  E  A  A  T  S  I  S  Ă  G  A  O  D
N  E  D  B  R  T  U  R  R  T  O  D  O  A  F  N
I  T  U  S  R  D  L  T  T  A  O  S  U  V  A  A
K  O  J  A  N  O  A  L  Î  O  V  L  Z  E  Î  T
O  L  Ă  I  B  L  V  N  E  T  C  E  O  A  N  S
S  O  F  T  F  E  C  A  P  S  N  L  L  V  Ţ  R
A  O  N  R  V  H  A  T  T  T  O  C  O  M  E  E
T  K  O  A  I  D  F  U  O  U  E  T  Î  S  L  D
G  F  H  D  C  S  O  J  W  H  T  K  Ţ  Ă  E  N
O  O  E  D  N  I  V  A  O  S  E  R  Ă  L  G  U
T  R  A  T  U  Ă  C  A  R  H  Y  L  V  T  E  O
T  H  T  H  M  O  H  G  K  K  A  E  P  S  O  T
I  B  U  I  A  T  O  K  U  P  O  U  T  B  T  T
```

TO CLOSE	A ÎNCHIDE
TO COME	A VENI
TO DO	A FACE
TO DRINK	A BEA
TO FIND	A GĂSI
TO HAVE	A AVEA
TO HELP	A AJUTA
TO LOOK FOR	A CĂUTA
TO LOVE	A IUBI
TO SELL	A VINDE
TO SPEAK	A VORBI
TO TAKE	A LUA
TO TRAVEL	A CĂLĂTORI
TO UNDERSTAND	A ÎNȚELEGE
TO WORK	A MUNCI

Languages typically have a mix of regular and irregular verbs. A regular verb has a predictable conjugation. An irregular verb has a conjugation that does not follow the typical pattern. In English, many of the most common verbs are irregular.

```
C O U N H T D A C U M P Ă R A E
I A C E L P A A L E R G A M D E
Î T O T V E Y Ț A Ș T I E T A D
Ă O A K N A T S Ă Ș R R H O T I
Ș W A M L H E I R V G H V O O H
Ț A O P E J V L R E N E N P R C
E N O E U R I Ț O W T Î R E A S
U T Ț C Î L G T F T O D A N C E
L M A C L A O E Ț O U T E D W D
Ă D S S O K T E I B Ț E L O A A
G Î H E N A L T N U Î T O N O T
E T P O V A S A N Y C T T H O W
N Ă W R B K D E W A Ș O O E T O
Q B E I R C S A H O R E O G E H
O A G W H Q Ș E H U T Ă Ș C O C
L S K R X Ș A E N Ș Î Ă N R E A
```

TO BUY	A CUMPĂRA
TO DANCE	A DANSA
TO GIVE	A DA
TO GO	A MERGE
TO KNOW	A ȘTI
TO LEARN	A ÎNVĂȚA
TO LEAVE	A PLECA
TO OPEN	A DESCHIDE
TO OWE	A DATORA
TO PLAY	A SE JUCA
TO RUN	A ALERGA
TO WALK	A MERGE
TO WANT	A VREA
TO WRITE	A SCRIE

FOOD 1

One of the greatures pleasures of travelling to another country is sampling the local cuisine. Study the word list below so you can order with confidence.

```
H H E X S Q C H O C O L A T E V
A T E D A X N T I S R U A D E C
E Ă L W A Â O O M U G E Ă D V A
S Q M L O R C S H N M W A T E R
U I I I O O Ă S Ă T A L A S G N
G U E Ă L P R H Ă R A O E V E E
A T S A P K X E X S B E A G T T
R E T S A P W W Z H H U G O A P
T Ă F T S S Â N I C O S T D B A
A Z L Â T D M B T F R U I T L L
G N O C A H R C N L E G U M E K
O Â U E A R X T D O I R R N S R
I R R S W F K X L T F Ă I N Ă A
F B K P H F K R A N H Â P C U N
T Ă T N E E T O R A P U I A E I
T J S A V E A T Z I N L A N V R
```

BREAD	PÂINE
BUTTER	UNT
CHEESE	BRÂNZĂ
CHOCOLATE	CIOCOLATĂ
EGGS	OUĂ
FLOUR	FĂINĂ
FRUIT	FRUCT
MEAT	CARNE
MILK	LAPTE
PASTA	PASTE
RICE	OREZ
SALAD	SALATĂ
SUGAR	ZAHĂR
VEGETABLES	LEGUME
WATER	APĂ

FOOD 2

Want more? You have quite an appetite (for learning). Feast on this delicious buffet of mouth watering words.

```
I  E  L  U  I  F  E  E  Î  P  H  A  S  A  E  G
S  U  A  A  Z  E  P  R  Ă  J  I  T  U  R  I  S
N  O  N  H  M  E  C  T  A  Ț  I  P  H  N  E  D
Ă  S  U  U  P  B  A  M  Ă  S  E  O  E  Î  Î  Ă
I  P  G  P  Î  Ț  S  Î  R  Î  I  T  R  R  C  F
Ț  O  E  E  E  K  H  T  N  Ț  R  T  E  H  A  T
F  R  Î  H  S  L  N  T  Î  L  E  E  I  S  R  L
E  K  G  Ț  P  U  I  T  Ă  N  Q  C  M  U  N  A
S  N  I  M  E  X  W  O  E  R  K  E  G  P  E  S
Î  P  I  Ț  A  T  S  R  E  E  B  O  P  Ă  D  R
O  Ă  Y  W  N  E  D  T  N  S  Y  B  E  R  E  Î
X  U  E  T  I  Ț  R  I  Ă  L  C  E  N  D  P  S
Ă  W  N  K  H  D  V  C  A  K  E  K  I  R  O  R
T  N  O  R  R  T  S  H  E  U  L  I  I  S  R  L
U  O  H  G  T  B  Î  Î  Î  C  R  D  M  M  C  I
C  B  C  A  R  N  E  D  E  V  I  T  Ă  E  A  L
```

BEEF	CARNE DE VITĂ
BEER	BERE
CAKE	TORT
CHICKEN	PUI
COOKIES	PRĂJITURI
HONEY	MIERE
ICE CREAM	ÎNGHEȚATĂ
LAMB	MIEL
OIL	ULEI
PEPPER	PIPER
PORK	CARNE DE PORC
SALT	SARE
SOUP	SUPĂ
WINE	VIN
YOGURT	IAURT

FRUIT 1

26

A fruit is the part of a plant that surrounds the seeds, whereas a vegetable is a plant that has some other edible part. Tomatoes, cucumbers and peppers are three examples of fruit that are often classified as vegetables.

Ă	E	Ă	S	Ă	I	E	V	Â	N	Ă	T	Ă	W	P	Â
M	L	R	J	G	N	Â	B	E	O	E	I	Â	M	Ă	L
S	E	A	Ă	S	V	I	V	A	L	P	N	S	D	M	C
T	A	P	C	T	U	R	F	P	E	R	G	P	Â	E	Ă
R	E	R	I	O	H	C	P	A	M	G	E	F	A	L	P
A	E	I	S	S	T	A	R	P	R	P	N	Ă	A	O	Ş
W	D	C	R	M	E	R	N	S	E	O	S	A	M	N	U
B	R	O	E	N	B	Ş	O	N	T	I	D	E	R	E	N
E	E	T	I	U	R	F	E	P	A	R	G	I	L	O	I
R	V	P	P	A	Ă	Ş	C	C	W	R	U	M	E	Ă	L
R	E	Ă	S	H	Ş	S	A	N	A	N	A	G	N	W	T
I	N	P	E	A	C	H	G	N	K	C	O	U	U	A	E
E	E	E	P	S	I	I	A	S	A	P	R	M	Ş	R	Ă
S	P	L	A	R	E	T	N	A	L	P	G	G	E	Ş	I
S	E	I	R	R	E	B	E	U	L	B	C	W	R	L	T
T	P	E	G	S	T	T	M	Ş	A	D	T	E	I	W	L

APRICOT	CAISĂ
BLUEBERRIES	AFINĂ
EGGPLANT	VÂNĂTĂ
GRAPEFRUIT	GREPFRUT
GRAPES	STRUGURI
LEMON	LĂMÂIE
MELON	PEPENE
ORANGE	PORTOCALĂ
PEACH	PIERSICĂ
PEAR	PARĂ
PINEAPPLE	ANANAS
PLUM	PRUNĂ
POMEGRANATE	RODIE
STRAWBERRIES	CĂPŞUNI
WATERMELON	PEPENE VERDE

28

There are more than 7000 different varieties of apples being grown around the world today. Check out our produce section below for some more fresh and tasty fruit.

```
Y  B  C  C  Â  C  Â  Ş  Â  I  Ă  L  Ş  L  T  E
E  A  A  H  Y  I  Â  Ă  N  N  E  L  I  Ă  M  Ş
L  N  N  E  D  R  E  V  I  E  D  R  A  M  G  E
L  A  T  R  W  A  E  H  S  A  U  Q  S  Â  E  R
O  N  A  R  R  R  C  P  Z  U  C  C  H  I  N  I
W  A  L  I  Ă  O  A  M  P  D  O  V  L  E  A  C
P  R  O  E  M  E  F  S  U  E  A  R  H  V  H  Ă
E  D  U  S  Ă  Ă  I  G  P  R  P  E  T  E  S  R
P  E  P  E  N  E  G  A  L  B  E  N  Ş  R  E  U
P  I  E  A  D  O  V  L  E  C  E  L  E  D  N  E
E  G  N  R  P  W  T  H  A  I  A  R  P  E  T  M
R  A  R  D  E  I  R  O  Ş  U  Ş  E  R  P  R  Z
B  L  S  U  N  I  K  P  M  U  P  O  L  I  A  G
W  B  N  B  D  Ă  V  R  X  P  H  T  R  V  E  V
I  E  B  L  A  C  K  B  E  R  R  I  E  S  O  S
W  N  U  H  H  N  A  R  T  O  M  A  T  O  L  D
```

APPLE	MĂR
BANANA	BANANĂ
BLACKBERRIES	MURE
CANTALOUPE	PEPENE GALBEN
CHERRIES	CIREŞE
FIG	SMOCHINĂ
GREEN PEPPER	ARDEI VERDE
LIME	LĂMÂIE VERDE
PUMPKIN	DOVLEAC
RASPBERRIES	ZMEURĂ
RED PEPPER	ARDEI ROŞU
SQUASH	DOVLEAC
TOMATO	ROŞIE
YELLOW PEPPER	ARDEI GALBEN
ZUCCHINI	DOVLECEL

A 2013 study estimated that up to 87% of people in the United States do no consume their daily recommended portion of vegetables. Here is a list of vegetables that you should probably be eating more of.

```
T K B E E T S N T U T L G Ă O Ț
V K A R E W O L F I L U A C S E
O A G L O S F E C L Ă T R S A D
C B A R E C S O K A Ă R L E L R
R K R W E P C P C O N U I Ă A E
O A F O I E T O A Ă H A C S T V
M P Ț N C N N R L R P C P I Ă E
E C A R R O T P E I A A I S V R
Ă C O S P I L O E B R N E T E Ă
H Ă U I R N U I B A P G G C R Z
P P D T K O O A G Ț S H Ă H D A
F Ă I W T R G U P H Y I L N E M
O O A R U E S Ț E L I N Ă K L L
Q I N T C E L E R Y V A R Z Ă E
S L S Ț H Ă B I F O T R A C P D
O U A R O P O T A T O E S N O L
```

ARTICHOKE	ANGHINARE
ASPARAGUS	SPARANGHEL
BEETS	SFECLĂ
BROCCOLI	BROCOLI
CABBAGE	VARZĂ
CARROT	MORCOV
CAULIFLOWER	CONOPIDĂ
CELERY	ȚELINĂ
GARLIC	USTUROI
GREEN PEAS	MAZĂRE VERDE
KALE	KALE
LETTUCE	SALATĂ VERDE
ONION	CEAPĂ
POTATOES	CARTOFI
SPINACH	SPANAC

There's no place like home. Below is a list of words that are related to house and home.

```
M K H A L O S B U S I D Ă B E Y
O B I T N E M A T R A P A A T L
O F E T C N S S N S W E L A T H
R A O N C T N E M T R A P A B R
G N E O L H D M M O W E N E N A
N F W Z R R E E Ă E O I D A O E
I I E A A H S N O I D R N S Z A
N H Ş G L J U T F D O Ă H D D J
I E W R A Y F E V O E T L T O C
D A E R N D R E M R I Ă N A A W
I T A I D E A E D M S C B S S B
E G A R A G G M S I Y U Ă E E C
S W L S I B E D F T L B C S I I
P E T E Ş I R E P O C A U T L R
Ă R V L I V I N G R O O M U T Z
Ă T F S N Z E R R L H S E E O H
```

APARTMENT	APARTAMENT
BASEMENT	SUBSOL
BATHROOM	BAIE
BED	PAT
BEDROOM	DORMITOR
DINING ROOM	SALĂ DE MESE
FENCE	GARD
GARAGE	GARAJ
HOUSE	CASĂ
KITCHEN	BUCĂTĂRIE
LAWN	GAZON
LIVING ROOM	SUFRAGERIE
ROOF	ACOPERIŞ
WINDOW	FEREASTRĂ

It is estimated that one tenth of all furniture purchased in Britain comes from IKEA. Perhaps you have assembled a few of these items yourself.

```
W A S H I N G M A C H I N E T A
F N L Ă C T N E M N V Ş Ă S A M
E A S T H A T F I B E Ş U E L E
M U U C A V E A U E R E D T Ă U
Ă E Ş C Ă A T T Ş E N R E O P S
G N C H E R H D Y I E P P O S W
Ă U I H U T I R M P R A E P E I
E T T C A N D E L A B R U M D M
E E E B S N Ş S C I R R Ş A Ă M
G L Ă L T I D S E L B A T L N I
R I E C A L P E R I F E A Ş I N
D O O O I O Y R L W N M P E Ş G
A T V I R O T A R I P S A H A P
A O W O S T U F B Ă E I L I M O
Ş T U S C Ă T O R D E R U F E O
E F H D R R R G Y A S Ă D A C L
```

BATHTUB	CADĂ
CARPET	COVOR
CHANDELIER	CANDELABRU
CURTAIN	PERDEA
DRESSER	DULAP
DRYER	USCĂTOR DE RUFE
FAUCET	ROBINET
FIREPLACE	ŞEMINEU
LAMP	LAMPĂ
SWIMMING POOL	PISCINĂ
STAIRS	SCĂRI
TABLE	MASĂ
TOILET	TOALETĂ
VACUUM	ASPIRATOR
WASHING MACHINE	MAŞINĂ DE SPĂLAT

Here is a list of some more common household items and modern conveniences. Search the grid for the words listed below

```
M Ț Ț I S R G L C U P T O R S H
Ț H Ă G A G E Ă O N M I R R O R
S Ț N Ș Y E U Ș A S A E L R N S
E C R G A N T K R I H C N L U H
S R E L W A O L N S R D H I O O
E E P I L T M E A I E L R A R W
S F L P L S Ă W B S S E A S I E
M R T O A I H T K G D Y S S B R
H I U C H S N H E I O E L C U Ț
T G W E I C P G G V R N T A S A
Ș E S D T A L I F T U M Ă U U I
R R H Ț L D R O T A L I T N E V
N A P U Ș F A A S T N H H H T Y M
E T D T U Q M O V E N C H C X Ș
R O G Ă D N I L G O T Ș L W S H
A R S P Ă L Ă T O R D E V A S E
```

CHAIR	SCAUN
CEILING FAN	VENTILATOR
CHIMNEY	HORN
CLOSET	DULAP
CRIB	PĂTUȚ DE COPIL
DESK	BIROU
DISHWASHER	SPĂLĂTOR DE VASE
HALLWAY	HOL
MATTRESS	SALTEA
MIRROR	OGLINDĂ
OVEN	CUPTOR
PILLOW	PERNĂ
REFRIGERATOR	FRIGIDER
SHOWER	DUȘ
SINK	CHIUVETĂ

Table setting etiquette dictates that the forks be placed on the left hand side of the plate and knives on the right. Here are some items that you might find on your table, probably in the wrong location.

```
P U S A Ă R U G N I L S G Ţ E Ş
D I L N M Ţ E G L W O B O I R K
O H P C K N I F E A G D A T R H
Ţ T V E I W L R U E S P O O N T
M O E C R O A A U R E S F Ţ C Ă
T L E Ţ E V R E Ş G C L V U Ş S
T C Ă T H Ă Ţ C F P N U Ţ C S A
A E Ă Ă C T S N A D E I L A Y M
B L Ţ N T T I H R S T P L I U E
L B A A I K A S F L T G P G Ţ D
E A S C P R L H U I E R A E D Ă
S T L A D S R E R N H Ţ O D R Ţ
P Ă N E L Ş T E I G Ţ L Ţ N A A
O L V F S A R W E U R G E N T F
O I Ă T L A S F Ş R E Ş N C S A
N O O P S A E T L Ă N L R T Ţ L
```

BOWL	CASTRON
FORK	FURCULIŢĂ
GLASS	STICLĂ
KNIFE	CUŢIT
MUG	CANĂ
NAPKIN	ŞERVEŢEL
PEPPER	PIPER
PITCHER	ULCIOR
PLATE	FARFURIE
SALT	SARE
SPOON	LINGURĂ
TABLECLOTH	FAŢĂ DE MASĂ
TABLESPOON	LINGURĂ
TEASPOON	LINGURIŢĂ
WINE GLASS	PAHAR DE VIN

Time to get out the tool box and do some repairs on our vocabulary. Try to hammer a few of these words and their translations into you brain.

```
N S C R E W D R I V E R A A B E
V S A E T Ş E L C Ţ I D R U P R
E R E D L U Ţ G N S Ş A R T H U
R E W D O Ă I Ş P Ş T U Ă S V L
U I A A B R Ă H A E Ş S T C I R
S L S L Ă T C I G U C T U A M E
A P H A A S B R R R Ş E N R S N
E A E U B Ă Ţ U E O U Ă D Ă U I
M S R N Ş R B W M I H B L T R B
E R C L C E H N M S O T Ş V D E
P P I U L I Ţ Ă A L L N Ţ F R A
A O O N I F L W H C N E R W I Ţ
T E I C Ă E N H N N O R V Ş L I
A Ţ P I A N C J T E N I V E L Ă
Ă Z E C N A R F E I E H C A L W
A R U L E T Ă D E M Ă S U R A T
```

BOLT	SURUB
DRILL	BURGHIU
HAMMER	CIOCAN
LADDER	SCARĂ
LEVEL	NIVELĂ
NAIL	CUI
NUT	PIULIŢĂ
PENCIL	CREION
PLIERS	CLEŞTE
SAW	FIERĂSTRĂU
SCREW	ŞURUB
SCREWDRIVER	ŞURUBELNIŢĂ
TAPE MEASURE	RULETĂ DE MĂSURAT
WASHER	ŞAIBĂ
WRENCH	CHEIE FRANCEZĂ

Globally there are 1.2 billion pairs of jeans sold annually. That is a lot of denim! Take a look at this list of other common articles of clothing.

```
E I A B E D T A L A H I T D Ă P
E Î N C Ă L Ţ Ă M I N T E T O A
L O Z S K C O S H O R T S H M N
E Ă F H H Ă P U L O V E R A S T
T E B O R H T A B E V S J I R A
E I R E E G T A S H Ţ I T N E L
I T Ş S L N A T V R P N Ţ Ă A O
H K F O A T H S E A R N R G X N
Ş C V P S M S T C I R B I Î T I
T E U Ă Ă E A D Ş A H C Î O M S
S N A N R E T J Î U R C E Ş N C
W T U D W Ş I E A U W F O M J U
T Ş N S Y A C H I P I U T R W R
I M Ş A E R U C O A T Ă A A W Ţ
A O T B P F E H Q R D V H Ţ T I
O L Ţ M A Ă O E E D W S L O U E
```

BATHROBE	HALAT DE BAIE
BELT	CUREA
COAT	HAINĂ
DRESS	ROCHIE
GLOVES	MĂNUŞI
HAT	CHIPIU
NECKTIE	CRAVATĂ
PAJAMAS	PIJAMA
PANTS	PANTALONI
SCARF	EŞARFĂ
SHOES	ÎNCĂLŢĂMINTE
SHORTS	PANTALONI SCURŢI
SOCKS	ŞOSETE
SWEATER	PULOVER
VEST	VESTĂ

More than 2 billion t-shirts are sold each year! How many of these other items can be found in your closet?

```
R W R I S T W A T C H I R E E O
H Î N O Ă S M B L R Ă U Ţ J T A
Î M L G N U R O E C Ş S T O O B
S B I M T Ă T I E C A L K C E N
V R R S Ţ H L A Ş P M A D L H O
N Ă O A I O S T Ă T Ă D O E I I
E C R N C D Î N W B C N M N G P
Â Ă G A E E E Ţ V O A A E J U A
T M A M E L L M A W X S O E L P
S I Â Ţ S W A E Z T V R A R B W
N N U A O E R D T I U S M I W S
Ă T A S U T I E N E C H Ţ E K F
T E L E T E R B D A Î I T I E A
S A O V J Î N R R N S R R T Ş H
U A E E I A B E D M U T S O C Z
F H W R D S R E D N E P S U S R
```

WRIST WATCH	CEAS DE MÂNĂ
BOOTS	CIZME
BOW TIE	PAPION
BRA	SUTIEN
BRACELET	BRĂŢARĂ
CLOTHING	ÎMBRĂCĂMINTE
JEANS	BLUGI
NECKLACE	COLIER
SANDALS	SANDALE
SHIRT	CĂMAŞĂ
SKIRT	FUSTĂ
SUIT	COSTUM
SUSPENDERS	BRETELE
SWIM SUIT	COSTUM DE BAIE
UNDERWEAR	LENJERIE

The majority of people take less than half an hour to get ready in the morning. Some can be ready in less than 5 minutes, whereas some take over an hour. Here is a list of things that might be a part of your morning routine.

```
R E N E T P E I P H S O R N R J
P R T P A U F E U S Ă E C N C U
E A R S E D R Z O U Y O M H O R
M P O E A F D L A R M A F D N Ă
U A B S U P F T D B C A E Ă T P
F S K M H L H R E H L O E R A E
R T E E A A I T I T D Ş A A C D
A Ă A T U A M A O O T A P T T R
P D N Ş H P J P R O D M Ă N L O
L E N T I L E A O T T P D E E T
D D Ţ N G T N A R O D O E D N Ă
R I M O U T H W A S H N G Ă S C
H N S M R O Z A R U L U U Ţ E S
A Ţ G M A P A R A T D E R A S U
L I P S T I C K P I G S Ă P U N
O R I Ţ N I D E D Ă Ţ U I R E P
```

COMB	PIEPTENE
CONTACT LENSES	LENTILE de contact
DENTAL FLOSS	AŢĂ DENTARĂ
DEODORANT	DEODORANT
HAIR DRYER	USCĂTOR DE PĂR
LIPSTICK	RUJ
MAKEUP	MACHIAJ
MOUTHWASH	APĂ DE GURĂ
PERFUME	PARFUM
RAZOR	APARAT DE RAS
SHAMPOO	ŞAMPON
SOAP	SĂPUN
TOOTHBRUSH	PERIUŢĂ DE DINŢI
TOOTHPASTE	PASTĂ DE DINŢI

Places to go and people to see. Here are some places that you might visit around town.

```
I L N L T M U Z E U B L A R M L
R E A S T U F D E P A I T U A O
E O S T U B I R O U R N E T G O
I E T U I P R E H P E S Ş A A H
P A A D O P E O O M U O C A Z C
M Ă D P O H S R T M P Ă O E I S
O V I A O P T R M U R B A R N T
P I O S I S A H I A E S L O U A
E Ţ N T E P T C G Ţ R S Ă P N S
D G A A E R I O A I Y K Ă O I T
E L D D E F O E F M L M E R V K
I C D I O R N A D F R E H T E R
Ţ T U U R Ş R O E E I I F A R M
A B L M W B S O F F I C E B S S
T R A I N S T A T I O N E T A Ş
S U P E R M A R K E T Ă U Ş L N
```

AIRPORT	AEROPORT
BAR	BAR
BRIDGE	POD
DEPARTMENT store	MAGAZIN UNIVERSAL
FARM	FERMĂ
FIRE STATION	STAŢIE DE POMPIERI
HOSPITAL	SPITAL
LIGHTHOUSE	FAR
MUSEUM	MUZEU
OFFICE	BIROU
POST OFFICE	OFICIU POŞTAL
SCHOOL	ŞCOALĂ
STADIUM	STADION
SUPERMARKET	SUPERMARKET
TRAIN STATION	GARĂ

The weekend is finally here. Where to you feel like going tonight? Here are some more places you can visit.

```
N S T E T A T I S R E V I N U B
O S Ă N A E N E F A C I E O A S
I A R M A G A Z I N H R A N T E
T H E Y Y R R I T I M I C B R C
A D H X C R U A S H U Ă Y E O Ț
T E D E A T A A O R R T I F P I
S K O L M Ă T T T O I C F L E E
E K P A R C S A E S A E T E R D
C Y R P A E E Y R M E H I T A E
I E R A H T R E R S E R P S H P
L Ă H O P O V A H A C C I A O O
O N T R H I F O T S R A R C U L
P E H Ț N L P E K T N B S T S I
L D I U N B R N Ă O O N I T E Ț
E S I O T I A T Ă R E P O L L I
L Ă Ț R L B H O T E L E S O D E
```

BANK	BANCĂ
CASTLE	CASTEL
CEMETARY	CIMITIR
COFFEE SHOP	CAFENEA
HARBOR	PORT
HOTEL	HOTEL
LIBRARY	BIBLIOTECĂ
OPERA HOUSE	OPERĂ
PARK	PARC
PHARMACY	FARMACIE
POLICE STATION	SECȚIE DE POLIȚIE
RESTAURANT	RESTAURANT
STORE	MAGAZIN
THEATER	TEATRU
UNIVERSITY	UNIVERSITATE

Road trip time! Hop in your car, turn up the music and hit the open road. Make sure you study this list of road worthy translations before heading out.

```
S S E M A F O R O E Ş I G M P A
T T R A F F I C S N G S M O U P
O R H C E Ă N I Ş A M O T T Ş A
L A A I U R N I S L T S O O N E
G D C F Ş E A O F O E B M R R I
N Ă C A F S L C C D U U I C A R
I C I R N I T I R Z R S O Y Z Ă
K U D T N O C O B A N U T C U N
R S E E D L T L P O P Ă M L E I
A E N N E A I M I S M E D E D Z
P N T T C I O M A G I O D N W N
P S Ă I Ş R A R F G H G T C A E
A U D N A C C I D E N T N U O B
S N O I T A T S S A G O C R A L
I I R A E S B E N Z I N Ă Ş Ă T
K C U R T E E R T S Y A W E N O
```

AUTOMOBILE	MAŞINĂ
ACCIDENT	ACCIDENT
BUS	AUTOBUZ
GAS STATION	BENZINĂRIE
GASOLINE	BENZINĂ
LANE	BANDĂ
MOTORCYCLE	MOTOCICLETĂ
ONE-WAY STREET	STRADĂ CU SENS UNIC
PARKING LOT	LOC DE PARCARE
ROAD	DRUM
STOP SIGN	INDICATOR DE STOP
TRAFFIC LIGHT	SEMAFOR
TRAFFIC	TRAFIC
TRUCK	CAMION

There are many interesting ways of getting from A to B. Which mode of transportation will you choose?

```
U V G S F N T A D Z U O R T E M
E I Ț I L O P E D Ă N I Ș A M A
R M E F T Ț O O A A Ș I U I A Ș
E N A L P R I A E E P T A B D I
T F A R C R E V O H O E I R C N
P A B E O E B N S B L C O U T Ă
O A T T T S A I U Ș I T R S C D
C T A P F C I Z C C C I E U I E
I S M O D I Ș L L Y E E K B S P
L U B C N C R E G Y C N Ț M J O
E B U I O G T E A O A L G A P M
T M L L I Ă O W T T R Ș E R W P
A A A E V N B H Y R R E F I D I
W R N H A U Ș A M B U L A N C E
B I Ț C S U B L O O H C S E A R
R N Ă C R A B O A T T Ț K E A I
```

AIRPLANE	AVION
AMBULANCE	**AMBULANȚĂ**
BICYCLE	**BICICLETĂ**
BOAT	**BARCĂ**
CANOE	CANOE
FERRY	BAC
FIRE TRUCK	**MAȘINĂ DE POMPIERI**
HELICOPTER	ELICOPTER
HOVERCRAFT	AEROGLISOR
POLICE CAR	**MAȘINĂ DE POLIȚIE**
SCHOOL BUS	**AUTOBUZ ȘCOLAR**
SUBMARINE	SUBMARIN
SUBWAY	METROU
TANK	TANC
TRAIN	TREN

Here are some popular languages from around the world. Maybe you already know one or two of them.

```
Ă B A R A G H H V M H E B R E W
Z L Ă E A A E H H S I N A P S R
E P O H W E R R J U I Ă N W E U
M O E I O E I A M P N R V Ă M S
A R M N N G P P B A F F Z G A Ă
N T O A G A O R M I N E R H N Z
T U O N N L P R Ă V C E N I T E
E G O E O D E S D N A Y R T E N
I H S N O G A Z A C A A F N I O
V E E G T S I R Ă G D E R A V P
Y Z R L T E F T I N G R E E K A
Ă Ă U I T A L I A N Ă T N R R J
R U S S I A N M I L H E C O O N
T I L H S I L O P E I O H K E C
A B H E L N R Y E B R A I C Ă R
P E S E U G U T R O P Ă N H L X
```

ARABIC	ARABĂ
ENGLISH	ENGLEZĂ
FRENCH	FRANCEZĂ
GERMAN	GERMANĂ
GREEK	GREACĂ
ITALIAN	ITALIANĂ
JAPANESE	JAPONEZĂ
KOREAN	COREEANĂ
MANDARIN	MANDARINĂ
POLISH	POLONEZĂ
PORTUGUESE	PORTUGHEZĂ
RUSSIAN	RUSĂ
SPANISH	SPANIOLĂ
HEBREW	EBRAICĂ
VIETNAMESE	VIETNAMEZĂ

PROFESSIONS

Statistics suggest that the average person may change careers 5-7 times in their lives.
Thinking about a change? Why not try one of these great professions?

```
V  R  R  P  E  L  E  C  T  R  I  C  I  A  N  L
B  R  E  C  I  F  F  O  E  C  I  L  O  P  Ă  I
U  R  T  A  I  H  I  S  P  R  O  T  C  A  H  E
C  P  N  S  X  C  L  R  I  R  N  U  R  S  E  C
Ă  S  E  W  I  F  S  E  E  F  E  H  C  T  O  T
T  Y  P  H  D  T  P  E  Ă  F  I  F  E  Ă  S  C
A  C  R  I  U  I  N  L  E  T  I  A  O  I  P  E
R  H  A  E  L  I  K  E  E  R  C  G  Ț  E  R  T
O  I  C  O  G  O  R  C  D  H  E  I  H  E  O  I
T  A  T  N  H  T  T  T  E  O  L  I  N  T  F  H
C  T  E  D  E  S  S  R  Ă  O  C  I  P  A  E  C
O  R  L  G  R  R  Ă  I  P  R  G  T  V  M  S  R
D  I  E  Ă  O  W  W  C  T  N  E  O  O  D  O  A
T  S  H  T  P  Ț  E  I  I  N  C  Ț  N  R  R  P
A  T  C  R  E  Y  W  A  L  A  E  W  A  J  L  C
S  A  S  I  S  T  E  N  T  M  E  D  I  C  A  L
```

ACTOR	ACTOR
ARCHITECT	ARHITECT
CARPENTER	DULGHER
CHEF	BUCĂTAR
DENTIST	DENTIST
DOCTOR	DOCTOR
ELECTRICIAN	ELECTRICIAN
ENGINEER	INGINER
FIRE FIGHTER	POMPIER
LAWYER	AVOCAT
NURSE	ASISTENT MEDICAL
PILOT	PILOT
POLICE OFFICER	POLIȚIST
PSYCHIATRIST	PSIHIATRU
TEACHER	PROFESOR

What did you want to be when you were growing up? Was it one of these professions?

```
H S A O M D E Ş T I I N Ţ Ă S F
D A N C E R O T A S N A D M Ş Ă
F Y R O T I O R C W S I A E A B
L T C S R T K I P E N H R C C U
O N A I T E E A R T I S T A C T
R A Ş R N N R L L I B A T N O C
A I N S T A L A T O R N I I U H
R C O I M I H R T A Ş R P C N E
N I S E S C S C O R O L I A T R
A T D I H I T T E S U R I G A E
I I U O U T S T S M E C E L N Z
C L I R T I E E B B I F E O T I
I O J P R L F E R S A C O Ş M R
Z P Ă O H O R A U N Ă G I R I F
U P L T R P B M S M U D F Ă P P
M F A P A R A M E D I C E Q Ă R
```

ACCOUNTANT	CONTABIL
ARTIST	ARTIST
ATHLETE	ATLET
BARBER	FRIZER
BUTCHER	MĂCELAR
DANCER	DANSATOR
FLORIST	FLORAR
MECHANIC	MECANIC
MUSICIAN	MUZICIAN
PARAMEDIC	PARAMEDIC
PLUMBER	INSTALATOR
POLITICIAN	POLITICIAN
PROFESSOR	PROFESOR
SCIENTIST	OM DE ŞTIINŢĂ
TAILOR	CROITOR

There are thousands of unique and challenging careers out there to choose from. See if you can locate the following careers in the grid below.

```
M  J  E  W  E  L  E  R  A  N  I  D  Ă  R  G  T
P  E  A  R  L  R  E  D  N  E  T  R  A  B  N  M
O  R  N  X  E  N  E  N  H  S  S  R  O  T  F  E
Ş  E  D  F  E  V  A  I  I  D  O  O  E  J  E  D
T  M  D  D  A  M  I  L  D  T  O  T  T  C  R  I
A  R  R  R  R  A  R  S  L  S  A  A  N  M  C
Ş  A  B  A  O  N  M  I  D  I  O  L  X  A  I  V
G  F  B  U  R  T  C  A  L  I  O  S  I  M  E  E
R  T  S  U  S  A  Ă  A  C  C  X  N  M  R  R  T
A  E  O  O  M  D  N  C  T  I  A  A  E  E  N  E
C  J  S  R  L  R  R  C  U  T  S  R  T  H  Ş  R
S  O  A  G  U  D  F  I  R  D  U  T  R  S  F  I
E  H  T  J  C  V  A  A  V  X  A  N  I  I  A  N
P  S  I  B  I  J  U  T  I  E  R  R  S  F  E  A
I  E  M  N  A  I  R  A  N  I  R  E  T  E  V  R
D  Z  U  B  O  T  U  A  E  D  R  E  F  O  Ş  O
```

BARTENDER	BARMAN
BUS DRIVER	ŞOFER DE AUTOBUZ
FARMER	FERMIER
FISHERMAN	PESCAR
GARDENER	GRĂDINAR
JEWELER	BIJUTIER
JOURNALIST	JURNALIST
MAIL CARRIER	POŞTAŞ
PHARMACIST	FARMACIST
SOLDIER	SOLDAT
TAXI DRIVER	TAXIMETRIST
TRANSLATOR	TRADUCĂTOR
VETERINARIAN	MEDIC VETERINAR

In 2015, the New Horizons spacecraft successfully completed the first flyby of dwarf planet Pluto.   There is still so much to see and explore in our own solar system. Here are some key words from our celestial backyard.

```
E V N N B E T H D U R A N U S H
D T F L I O T U X I A D T C I F
H K E N U E Â D R M O A J O S E
S I T M V N E G I C O R T M T W
M J S E O S A L R O M O E E E W
E O Â D E C R A T E R R N T M Â
T O L P L U T O R E C E U Ă S E
S O C L N E H C T U C T T I O A
Y U W U R E U I R W N I P S L S
S U N T S R P Y T Â H P E A A E
R U S O I U T T M E E U N T R R
A F N E J O N Ă U E T J U U E L
L E G E M T P A S N W R N R R Ă
O C E H V T T E R Â N H A N E Ă
S U N E V H A F A U Â O E M E Q
R H Â H D E O Â M L S T T G E O
```

SOLAR SYSTEM	SISTEM SOLAR
MERCURY	MERCUR
VENUS	VENUS
EARTH	PĂMÂNT
MOON	LUNA
MARS	MARTE
JUPITER	JUPITER
SATURN	SATURN
URANUS	URANUS
NEPTUNE	NEPTUN
PLUTO	PLUTO
SUN	SOARE
CRATER	CRATER
ASTEROID	ASTEROID
COMET	COMETĂ

Here are some musical instruments to get your foot tapping and your hands clapping.

```
T  S  Ă  B  U  T  E  E  H  T  N  V  T  D  I  P
E  E  T  U  L  F  U  D  N  T  P  I  Y  Ţ  R  Ă
G  N  I  R  Ă  P  S  A  X  O  F  O  N  A  I  P
V  I  O  L  O  N  C  E  L  E  U  A  H  E  I  R
E  R  P  H  I  M  I  H  P  F  O  R  E  C  I  A
Ă  U  M  D  P  N  B  R  I  I  E  Ă  R  E  B  H
R  O  I  A  N  O  C  O  U  T  P  R  S  U  V  D
T  B  C  E  S  E  X  E  N  B  A  G  T  I  R  H
U  M  E  E  L  D  T  A  Ă  E  M  R  A  A  M  A
A  A  E  L  T  R  T  Ţ  S  N  U  A  Ă  B  N  R
E  T  O  T  O  O  U  Ă  V  M  W  D  T  H  R  M
Ă  I  O  M  O  C  B  A  P  I  U  I  Z  O  I  O
V  E  B  S  I  A  T  E  P  M  O  R  T  E  Ţ  N
F  O  A  Z  R  A  T  I  U  G  T  L  D  S  D  I
N  C  U  A  N  U  O  Q  G  D  E  P  I  A  N  C
S  M  N  O  I  D  R  O  C  C  A  T  O  N  A  A
```

ACCORDION	ACORDEON
BAGPIPES	CIMPOI
CELLO	VIOLONCEL
DRUMS	TOBE
FLUTE	FLAUT
GUITAR	CHITARĂ
HARMONICA	MUZICUŢĂ
HARP	HARPĂ
PIANO	PIAN
SAXOPHONE	SAXOFON
TAMBOURINE	TAMBURINĂ
TROMBONE	TROMBON
TRUMPET	TROMPETA
TUBA	TUBĂ
VIOLIN	VIOARĂ

This puzzle might make you happy, angry, or maybe even a little confused. See if you can complete this very emotional puzzle by finding all of the words in the grid.

```
X Ț Ă H H F Î N G R I J O R A T
M Â N D R U N I A G I T A T A I
O E O D I R C X R Î P T N T H M
T S D E S I R P R U S E I N R I
A A T T G O E I L E D C T E H D
M D N S R S Z C I I I N D R Î S
S L E I T H Ă O F R C E V V H I
A V Î T Ș Y T N E C R T G O Â Ș
I A Î O I U O F T A A H I U Ă R
Z U F N O C R U C I E W A S R O
U Î P A U A X S R D O M L P I E
T N O I T O M E A R E T O T P T
N O M Ă P R P D R N O R Ș Ț R Y
E I I D A S I I N Â G Ț O V I L
T P R O U D E S S A R R A B M E
O D Ă J D D R Ț T L V T Y N T I
```

EMOTION	EMOȚIE
HAPPY	FERICIT
SAD	TRIST
EXCITED	ENTUZIASMAT
BORED	PLICTISIT
SURPRISED	UIMIT
SCARED	SPERIAT
ANGRY	FURIOS
CONFUSED	CONFUZ
WORRIED	ÎNGRIJORAT
NERVOUS	AGITAT
PROUD	MÂNDRU
CONFIDENT	ÎNCREZĂTOR
EMBARRASSED	RUȘINAT
SHY	TIMID

If you are feeling any symptoms of the following conditions it might be time to visit the doctor. When you are feeling better the words below are waiting to be found.

```
F Ă V C H E A D A C H E G Ă E R
O L N O R B I I Ă I H V I D Ă F
C A U E F A N J D Ţ C R A M P E
R Z A E B F A I D I A B E T I B
A A U E E L A W I C R E E L R R
M N T C L R Ţ N E C N E R Ţ G Ă
P E Ţ E R Ă F A A O I E A G D S
S I R H W E L E S U S I S B M V
E G E T C Ă S E E G E G H U D O
Y A Ă T T U B R C H K R S N T C
O R I M A L T A V I O E D T F Ţ
X O P N E K C I H C R L P E N E
N M D E H Z I D T Ţ T A V T P O
H E D D L O C M I R S E V Ă I R
S H P A C E D E R E R U D A L R
L A R B E R E C R A L U C S A V
```

ALLERGY	ALERGIE
CHICKENPOX	VARICELĂ
COLD	RACEALĂ
COUGH	TUSE
CRAMPS	CRAMPE
DIABETES	DIABET
DIARRHEA	DIAREE
FEVER	FEBRĂ
FLU	GRIPĂ
HEADACHE	DURERE DE CAP
INFECTION	INFECŢIE
NAUSEA	GREAŢĂ
NOSEBLEED	HEMORAGIE NAZALĂ
RASH	ECZEMĂ
STROKE	accident VASCULAR CEREBRAL

Study these maladies so you can develop a healthy bilingual vocabulary.

```
O H X T M F R A C T U R E I T R
L K C A T T A T R A E H C Q P Ă
D O H R S C T S A C C I D E N T
A J S S A B R F T A N O I E R O
E Q C U U O R A H H T Â R Ă T E
N Â O R R A L C F N M G O L Ă R
T N N Ă C I A E E N I A R G I M
O E C T E M V D I M I O P C E I
R E U E O J I T S A U T O B T O
S R S T P C O P P M T M L A U F
Ă A S I C I R H E I O Ă P N R B
V J I A U A L A L Ţ A A N S Ă E
R O O S I R S E I O A T T Â M S
I P N N N L B E P I T N T U V B
E D U R E R I D E S T O M A C M
A E B S U R I V L P Y A U F Ă M
```

ACCIDENT	ACCIDENT
ASTHMA	ASTM
BRUISE	VÂNĂTAIE
BURN	ARSURĂ
CONCUSSION	COMOŢIE
CUT	TĂIETURĂ
EPILEPSY	EPILEPSIE
FRACTURE	FRACTURĂ
HEART ATTACK	INFARCT
MEASLES	POJAR
MIGRAINE	MIGRENĂ
MUMPS	OREION
SPRAIN	ENTORSĂ
STOMACH ACHE	DURERI DE STOMAC
VIRUS	VIRUS

Here are some basic questions and terms that you might hear frequently used in any language. Why? Because. Find these questionable terms and phrases below.

```
C  Â  T  E  S  T  E  C  E  A  S  U  L  F  S  S
C  O  N  I  T  B  P  R  B  R  N  O  Â  T  E  C
A  K  Ţ  I  S  R  E  Â  A  E  T  U  A  H  Â  H
N  C  V  N  A  I  A  C  L  F  O  H  W  T  I  Â
Y  Y  W  H  E  R  E  P  A  Y  W  N  C  R  C  H
O  E  N  I  C  T  A  M  E  U  Â  O  W  C  A  Y
U  H  Ţ  P  E  E  O  R  I  D  S  H  H  Ţ  F  I
H  C  E  C  R  S  A  O  V  T  E  E  R  A  I  S
E  U  U  R  A  W  T  Ă  Ă  E  T  D  E  A  A  A
L  M  Ă  P  O  Ţ  I  A  J  U  T  A  T  C  M  V
P  W  O  H  E  Ă  R  B  R  N  O  U  H  Â  E  Q
M  O  H  I  D  D  E  R  W  U  L  K  Ă  W  C  D
E  H  N  E  E  O  N  I  O  Â  J  H  H  N  Â  N
N  F  L  F  N  F  V  U  S  V  H  Y  X  Â  N  E
B  Q  E  R  T  T  I  H  G  Ţ  O  T  E  D  D  L
H  A  O  D  I  T  S  U  D  A  I  W  O  E  Ă  D
```

BECAUSE	DEOARECE
HOW	CUM
HOW ARE YOU	CE MAI FACI
HOW FAR	CÂT DE DEPARTE
HOW MUCH	CÂT COSTĂ
CAN YOU HELP ME	MĂ POŢI AJUTA
WHAT	CE
WHAT TIME IS IT	CÂT ESTE CEASUL
WHEN	CÂND
WHERE	UNDE
WHO	CINE
WHY	DE CE

Table for two? Welcome to our Learn with Word Search restaurant. On the menu are the following helpful and delicious restaurant related words. Enjoy!

```
Ş E R V E Ţ E L E Ş I Ş C A B E
E F E E T S A F M Â I T H E H N
O E N Ţ S O P I A I M Ş E I M H
O L N O I T E S I C C E L E L S
Ă U I B L S R E N D T D N O Â A
O L D Ă E A I O C I E U E I R Â
U P W U N F T S O I K S R J U A
C R M T I K I N U M N P E Ă U C
K I A U W A V L R O S Ă A R H N
Z N Â R P E D A S A M E P N T Â
W C I Ă Y R T H E B I L L R C M
A I E R G B E A T O A L E T Ă A
G P Â I D E Ş N N I I S U I R N
Ţ A P P E T I Z E R S A P N I L
S L W V I W A I T E R I S H C R
E I R U N I V E D Ă T S I L F H
```

APPETIZER	APERITIV
BREAKFAST	MIC DEJUN
DESSERT	DESERT
DINNER	CINĂ
DRINK	BĂUTURĂ
EAT	A MÂNCA
LUNCH	MASA DE PRÂNZ
MAIN COURSE	FELUL PRINCIPAL
MENU	MENIU
NAPKINS	ŞERVEŢELE
RESTROOMS	TOALETĂ
THE BILL	FACTURĂ
TIP	BACŞIŞ
WAITER	CHELNER
WINE LIST	LISTĂ DE VINURI

After that delicious meal it is time to head back to the hotel and relax. Here is a list of hotel words that might help give you a good night's sleep.

```
E Ă C I N E I G I E I T R Â H Ţ
Ă B R U T S I D T O N O D D O W
Z R M N E A N N R O O M B O T O
E O E O O A J E T D Z L A H E R
S A F C E I C N L E Y N G Ţ L E
S S Y E E E S U A H R I A W L P
Y C V C P P G I A R H N J T I A
N A B Ţ O G T Z V E E O E N O P
E M I S A O N I C E A D T T R T
T E O G W E R V O H L E U E T E
B R E E Y U N E F N R E I N L L
P Ă L R T M B L A N K E T S U I
W D S Ă E J Ă E E F H F I Â X O
W A P A T Ă E T Y C A N V D E T
S I Â S A L Ă D E F I T N E S S
H I H N S Z Y W K E Â N I B J E
```

BED	PAT
BLANKETS	PĂTURI
DO NOT DISTURB	NU DERANJATI
GYM	SALĂ DE FITNESS
HOTEL	HOTEL
INTERNET	INTERNET
KEY	CHEIE
LUGGAGE	BAGAJE
RECEPTION	RECEPŢIE
ROOM	CAMERĂ
TELEVISION	TELEVIZIUNE
TOILET PAPER	HÂRTIE IGIENICĂ
TOWEL	PROSOP

Were you a good student?   Here are some subjects that you may have studied long ago, or may be learning right now. Study these challenging subject translations.

```
H  J  E  G  E  A  P  I  P  E  Ş  G  O  B  W  Q
F  D  B  C  Ţ  C  B  H  Y  Ă  Ţ  N  I  I  T  Ş
G  E  U  E  O  M  N  H  Y  G  Z  E  Ă  O  J  U
N  T  S  N  I  N  A  E  S  S  O  N  A  L  I  U
I  F  I  L  O  Z  O  F  I  E  I  L  Ş  O  C  T
R  E  N  T  A  B  R  M  A  C  I  C  O  G  L  E
E  Ă  E  C  O  N  O  M  I  C  S  R  S  I  M  M
E  C  S  H  H  Y  G  D  H  E  E  I  O  E  B  M
N  I  S  I  U  E  E  U  Ă  I  N  R  D  T  Y  U
I  T  X  M  E  M  M  C  A  G  S  I  I  A  S  Z
G  A  E  I  E  U  I  I  I  G  C  T  E  R  Ă  I
N  M  Ţ  E  S  Z  M  N  S  I  E  N  O  T  Ş  C
E  E  S  I  I  A  E  E  N  T  U  S  R  R  D  Ă
I  T  C  F  T  R  G  E  O  G  R  A  P  H  Y  Ş
T  A  P  H  I  L  O  S  O  P  H  Y  E  L  E  E
E  M  Ă  E  I  F  A  R  G  O  E  G  L  A  V  R
```

ART	ARTĂ
BIOLOGY	BIOLOGIE
BUSINESS	AFACERI
CHEMISTRY	CHIMIE
ECONOMICS	ECONOMIE
ENGINEERING	INGINERIE
GEOGRAPHY	GEOGRAFIE
HISTORY	ISTORIE
LANGUAGES	LIMBI
MATH	MATEMATICĂ
MEDICINE	MEDICINĂ
MUSIC	MUZICĂ
PHILOSOPHY	FILOZOFIE
PHYSICS	FIZICĂ
SCIENCE	ŞTIINŢĂ

Math. Some people love it, and some people hate it. Add these words to your vocabulary and multiply your language skills.

```
E Ă S N O I T C A R T B U S A T
F A D U N A R E I Ţ A U C E B Ţ
E R I Ţ L U M N Î I A T Ă R Ţ P
Q A V R P Î Ţ Ţ E D D N W Î O E
U L I V I A C I D Ţ O E P G V R
A U S O R V R I U Z M C E Ă U P
T C I L Z T T A T U A O R N N E
I I O U E I D P L E M R C I O N
O D N M O T A O F E M P E I I D
N N O N E R V R T N L H N A T I
S E A U A T A R I T M E T I C C
G P A L Ă C Y Ţ Q G J P A I A U
A R L S Ţ T H T I P L S G V R L
E E R I Ţ R Ă P M Î Ţ Ă E T F A
L P E R E D Ă C S Ţ Ă R U L E R
N O I T A C I L P I T L U M L T
```

ADDITION	ADUNARE
AREA	ZONĂ
ARITHMETIC	ARITMETIC
DIVISION	ÎMPĂRŢIRE
EQUATION	ECUAŢIE
FRACTION	FRACŢIE
GEOMETRY	GEOMETRIE
MULTIPLICATION	ÎNMULŢIRE
PARALLEL	PARALEL
PERCENTAGE	PROCENT
PERPENDICULAR	PERPENDICULAR
RULER	RIGLĂ
SUBTRACTION	SCĂDERE
VOLUME	VOLUM

It is estimated that globally there are over 100,000 flights per day. Here are some common airport related terms for you to learn while they try to find your lost baggage.

```
I  I  Ă  S  T  L  A  M  A  V  T  C  N  U  P  L
I  N  T  E  R  N  A  Ţ  I  O  N  A  L  E  I  A
B  H  R  C  O  L  A  N  I  M  R  E  T  F  S  N
M  O  A  U  P  L  E  C  Ă  R  I  R  F  G  T  O
D  A  O  R  A  H  A  T  I  G  U  O  T  F  Ă  I
E  Q  P  I  Ş  R  E  V  Ţ  N  E  E  A  Z  D  T
P  A  D  T  A  Ă  A  O  W  K  K  R  H  D  E  A
A  C  R  A  P  L  I  A  A  C  C  T  E  F  D  N
R  U  D  T  S  Ă  Y  T  I  R  U  C  E  S  E  R
T  S  S  E  R  E  V  T  I  R  I  S  O  S  C  E
U  T  M  R  C  O  P  A  S  S  P  O  R  T  O  T
R  O  C  M  S  O  P  T  N  E  Y  O  E  W  L  N
E  M  P  I  O  O  L  O  E  O  E  A  R  E  A  I
S  S  U  N  E  C  V  A  R  L  R  T  N  T  R  R
O  E  G  A  G  G  A  B  R  E  I  E  A  D  E  A
T  T  Ş  L  V  S  P  E  A  E  A  B  A  G  A  J
```

AIRCRAFT	AERONAVĂ
AIRPORT	AEROPORT
ARRIVALS	SOSIRI
BAGGAGE	BAGAJ
CUSTOMS	PUNCT VAMAL
DEPARTURES	PLECĂRI
GATE	POARTĂ
INTERNATIONAL	INTERNAŢIONALE
PASSPORT	PAŞAPORT
RUNWAY	PISTĂ DE DECOLARE
SECURITY	SECURITATE
TAKEOFF	DECOLARE
TERMINAL	TERMINAL
TICKET	BILET

Farming has existed since 10,000 BC. If you work on a farm, or just like eating food, here are a some farm words for you harvest.

```
W D A Ă Y F Q O Ş O I L Y S H Ă
B V M Ă V R T S D E D Ă Ă T Ţ C
T E D E O L Ş T H E C H Ă A D H
R R L C N L C H E A E O R U O I
A R A Ş T A D G V U N A C R U C
C L I C P A D Ă A D E K S O L K
T I Ş R T D B S P N T E H J Ş E
O J Ă O C O W Ţ B U L L W S Ş N
R I I P L N R Ţ R R I C N E G Ş
E B Ă S E K P K B H Ă H F W Ă E
I P M R I E E Ş I N Ă F Ă R A T
M N A A M Y H O E G B N N H Ă Ă
R G S G L Ţ A S C X O A B V Z E
E O C Ă A I O E S R A N D G P A
F A R M E R E T S O O R I W T O
C T Ă T L O C E R T V P T Z E O
```

BULL	TAUR
CHICKEN	PUI
COW	VACĂ
CROPS	RECOLTĂ
DONKEY	MĂGAR
DUCK	RAŢĂ
FARMER	FERMIER
GOAT	CAPRĂ
HORSE	CAL
LAMB	MIEL
PIG	PORC
ROOSTER	COCOŞ
SHEEP	OAIE
TRACTOR	TRACTOR
TURKEY	CURCAN

Time to get out there and experience all there is to see. How do you prefer to explore a new city? Try exploring these highly rated sightseeing words.

```
H S U V E N I R U R I E A P E O
I I G H I D T U R I S T I C M E
Ă I S H G D R I S N I U R I O D
Ă I R O I U E I Ț A M R O F N I
T Ă R N U D I O R E N I U R U U
R E W E S V C D C I H S M I M G
A H I Y D I E I E A B T N H E R
E A M R R R W N E B M F P A N U
D P O U A E O I I A O E A R T O
E N N L S C L C T R O O R T E T
I I U E A E R L M P S Q K Ă I O
R D M M E A U A A A Ă M U Z E U
E I E H Ț E T M P G C O T M W R
L R N G I I Ț C A R T A I P H I
A D T Ț O O T O F T A R A P A S
G Ă S N O I T C A R T T A G G T
```

ART GALLERY	GALERIE DE ARTĂ
ATTRACTIONS	ATRACȚII
CAMCORDER	VIDEOCAMERĂ
CAMERA	APARAT FOTO
GUIDE BOOK	GHID
INFORMATION	INFORMAȚIE
MAP	HARTĂ
MONUMENTS	MONUMENTE
MUSEUM	MUZEU
PARK	PARC
RUINS	RUINE
SOUVENIRS	SUVENIRURI
TOUR GUIDE	GHID TURISTIC
TOURIST	TURIST

Time to hit the beach for some sun, sand and surf. Below you will find a list of warm beach related words.

```
Ă T W S A N D C A S T L E A O Ă
O C H E L A R I D E S O A R E R
B T O N Î O A A Ă S G D H A T A
E E A A C G U B M S U I N Y C L
Ă T A E L Ă G L Ţ A E R H A A O
I Z A C O Ţ E I E L V U F A S S
G N E O H V F S G G G L Z W T E
Ă T A P O L I B N N A A A E E I
J D H H I O L A I U N V K S L Ţ
A R S W D F I M F S E C S T D C
L I O E Ă Ţ M Î R S U L T U E E
P M A R E I N A U B A A Ţ W N T
F I R Ă W B N I S I P T E U I O
N X E S J Î N E E R C S N U S R
R N T N E Y F R R Y E N M S I P
O W L A F Ţ T E E I R Ă L Ă P Ţ
```

BEACH	PLAJĂ
BUCKET	GĂLEATĂ
HAT	PĂLĂRIE
LIFE GUARD	SALVAMAR
OCEAN	OCEAN
SAND	NISIP
SANDCASTLE	CASTEL DE NISIP
SEA	MARE
SHOVEL	LOPATĂ
SUN	SOARE
SUNGLASSES	OCHELARI DE SOARE
SUNSCREEN	PROTECŢIE SOLARĂ
SURFING	SURF
SWIMMING	ÎNOT
WAVES	VALURI

Is the museum near or far? Is it expensive to get in or not? Start studying these opposite terms, and you may find out.

```
T S T E O E S B U Î C D A B F W
S N N N I E Î I E S S E R T S A
U A O O U D Ă L O R C L L A M S
G R A L S H U R Q Ă U A Î A H C
N R A T R C A T B U N O T O W Ă
Î O E B A Q C D D Î D M R O O Z
W W I U E Ă M I H E A T A L L U
H G I H D R R O M S L F A R T T
G O O D R Y A U M A O O H I E D
Ă O R R E C I O N O R S P T A A
S E E R W L E Î W T S E I O E N
N R T I R A K O W T I H A O A S
C B Z P O A D A D N E A I L N E
U S T B Î S I T U T Î L E S T A
N H L Î N Z R Q V M H I A H D W
H T Z Î Î R R E A Ă I D Z G V E
```

BIG	MARE
SMALL	MIC
WIDE	LARG
NARROW	ÎNGUST
TALL	ÎNALT
SHORT	SCUND
HIGH	ÎNALT
LOW	SCĂZUT
GOOD	BUN
BAD	RĂU
WET	UMED
DRY	USCAT
HARD	GREU
SOFT	MOALE

Would you be opposed or in favor of some more
opposite words?   For better or worse, here
are some more words to study and find.

```
E T N I B R E I F S G H Q E O Ş
Z L Î W I G N O Q Ş A T X E E I
G S I G R A D R U M E N I Ş C R
O G H E B O S E I D L Ş C N S C
M T Ş E N Î N C E T R L L A U H
O I R A L N N G T N A E E R T K
T E E X Y E Î Î S S I S A L T E
O E T T W F Î C I X Ş T N P I D
S V R O O S L L J U K D F N T U
Q I L E H C I T A H D I F E Ş A
D S N N H U S Ş R E C E A P I F
F N D E S M T Î N C H I S O N H
I E A Y I P I N T O E E T O I A
T P F J V V H N T D I P A R L R
S X Î K W D T W Ş I W S D L O C
D E S C H I S W A T I L Y T Ş O
```

FAST	RAPID
SLOW	ÎNCET
RIGHT	DREAPTA
WRONG	GREŞIT
CLEAN	CURAT
DIRTY	MURDAR
QUIET	LINIŞTIT
NOISY	ZGOMOTOS
EXPENSIVE	SCUMP
CHEAP	IEFTIN
HOT	FIERBINTE
COLD	RECE
OPEN	DESCHIS
CLOSED	ÎNCHIS

They say that opposites attract. See if you are attracted to the list of opposite words below. Find them in the grid, or don't.

```
I  Y  D  D  N  Î  F  Ş  Î  R  H  H  E  Ş  L  Â
Q  B  Ş  A  L  A  D  N  I  C  O  G  L  P  X  T
N  E  N  Â  T  I  A  Ţ  V  H  H  I  G  F  M  X
H  G  Ţ  H  D  S  S  T  Î  N  C  E  P  U  T  E
G  I  I  Ş  Î  G  H  H  Â  I  N  E  Ş  L  I  A
Î  N  E  D  Â  H  F  G  F  S  Ş  O  V  L  Ş  Ţ
C  N  S  Î  N  C  H  I  S  A  R  E  U  A  R  Ş
S  I  H  C  S  E  D  L  E  A  A  T  E  M  Â  Q
L  N  N  Q  B  O  H  T  A  Y  J  M  Ş  A  F  J
A  G  E  R  I  Ţ  B  U  S  T  R  O  N  G  S  C
B  A  W  V  E  D  K  A  E  W  N  Ş  E  O  D  Â
O  A  B  Ş  W  T  E  S  S  I  Â  Â  L  L  T  D
O  A  X  P  Q  Î  U  U  L  O  A  U  G  M  K  N
A  I  E  E  C  Y  T  P  M  E  V  H  O  R  R  Ţ
I  Ş  H  O  N  I  M  Î  I  Ţ  S  W  N  L  A  W
T  I  A  G  G  O  T  L  U  C  I  F  F  I  D  S
```

FULL	PLIN
EMPTY	GOL
NEW	NOU
OLD	VECHI
LIGHT	DESCHIS
DARK	ÎNCHIS
EASY	UŞOR
DIFFICULT	DIFICIL
STRONG	PUTERNIC
WEAK	SLAB
FAT	GRAS
THIN	SUBŢIRE
BEGINNING	ÎNCEPUT
END	SFÂRŞIT

An antonym is a word opposite in meaning to another. A synonym is a word that has the same or similar meaning to another word. Find the antonyms from the word list in the puzzle grid.

```
A O E O L I Â O A Â D E E U A U
Ă W I H H Ă H T Ă H I H I C D L
E A S Â X Â Â R I A A D D R R R
C R Â D T B T F H E R E B U D R
Î P L H T N T E I C P P E C P Ă
O A O S Y O O F Ă R Ă A F A R Ă
G M O W F L Î N I A S R O E M U
Q I H G O S R M L E T T R R H Î
A R M C D C U A N N O E E R P N
U Ă A E A L T L E M E R V E D A
Î T K F E E U O A R A K T D I I
R Â I E Ă M A L E D I S N I M N
Ă R V E I F A H A E C C T S B T
T Z D T T H T I W S I Â E T O E
S I L E Î O T I W I T H O U T D
X U R T N U Ă N Î T I I E O Ă E
```

NEAR	APROAPE
FAR	DEPARTE
HERE	AICI
THERE	ACOLO
WITH	CU
WITHOUT	FĂRĂ
BEFORE	ÎNAINTE DE
AFTER	DUPĂ
EARLY	DEVREME
LATE	TÂRZIU
INSIDE	ÎNĂUNTRU
OUTSIDE	AFARĂ
FIRST	PRIMUL
LAST	ULTIMUL

We encounter many different materials on a
daily basis. Some are strong enough to hold
up buildings and others are soft and flexible.
Here is a list of common materials to choose
from as we continue to build your language
skills.

```
Ă L T K Y T C L Ţ M L C A E T S
S Y E N S D E R U C I T S A L P
R C R P I S I N T T N M B M L A
T T A E C G Y A S A A E V A A W
L G G N V P R A M G T O T T I S
C D O O W L L A L O Ă I W E R P
Z C Ţ T L P I A N R N S A R E T
N O E S Y D S S T U T D T I T U
A N L X L S A A M I K R R A A A
V C Ă L P N I L C E N F G L M E
R R Ă E D P Y L A S T Ă H Ţ E B
I E D Y E U Ă E N T P A C E X C
R T P R Ţ R L M S T E E L S Ţ D
M E X P F P N N Ţ R T M A U L C
H Q T N O U T R Y S E U Y B D S
Ă T S H I C L Ă T F R N F D Q D
```

CLAY	LUT
CONCRETE	BETON
COPPER	CUPRU
DIAMOND	DIAMANT
GLASS	STICLĂ
GOLD	AUR
MATERIAL	MATERIAL
METAL	METAL
PLASTIC	PLASTIC
PLATINUM	PLATINĂ
SAND	NISIP
SILVER	ARGINT
STEEL	OŢEL
STONE	PIATRĂ
WOOD	LEMN

See if you can handle another shipment of common materials. Be sure to handle each one with care.

```
L R H O N R F A T H O Â C N T A
E O O Ţ E L I N O X I D A B I L
E B S I Ă D P N M F A R B Ţ T U
T E F U D A E L Â A E T M R A M
S I C O T T O N U P R Ţ U T N I
S M T Ă R U M R A M S B B Ţ H N
S J N A R V N P M Ţ B S L C H U
E E E E N Ă J O R E H T A E L M
L E M Ţ C I M A R E C C A R E Ţ
N N E Y E I U I N I M U L A B E
I H C I N S M M D E I I A M R O
A G H A T I R E S Ă L C M I I O
T I V F T R L U N Â O U Ă C C O
S O I L S E Â Ă E T Ă A I Ă K E
T S H L I I Y H D T D C I Â A M
N R A P Â E Â O Y T A O Ţ D E A
```

ALUMINUM	ALUMINIU
BRASS	ALAMĂ
BRICK	CĂRĂMIDĂ
CEMENT	CIMENT
CERAMIC	CERAMICĂ
COTTON	BUMBAC
IRON	FIER
LEAD	PLUMB
LEATHER	PIELE
MARBLE	MARMURĂ
PAPER	HÂRTIE
RUBBER	CAUCIUC
SOIL	SOL
STAINLESS STEEL	OŢEL INOXIDABIL
TITANIUM	TITAN

We've made it through the first half of the book. Time to stop and have something to drink. Can we suggest one of the following?

```
Q W H I S K E Y E A D M T W L D
V N L E G O N I C C U P P A C F
A O A O A Y I S I E V N P T O Ă
T G D R E D W I N E E T O E F Y
R O M C A F E A A T E A O R F Y
V N Y N Ă R T V O E E I S Z E E
S I D K E O I E O U C D C E E H
A C N B S N H J N D F H U A S Y
E C A R A I W U Z E K S N N Y R
S U R L O G H T T O E A T A C I
C P B Ă L Ş O W U B C D G R W L
S P P E C I U J E O D Ă S X T T
Ş A M P A N I E N I R H T H L S
W C I A S I R I X U T Y I M F I
S U L E N G A P M A H C A N H W
E S K S E C E O E N E E M H H K
```

BEER	BERE
BRANDY	CONIAC
CAPPUCCINO	CAPPUCCINO
CHAMPAGNE	ŞAMPANIE
COFFEE	CAFEA
GIN	GIN
JUICE	SUC
MILK	LAPTE
RED WINE	VIN ROŞU
RUM	ROM
TEA	CEAI
VODKA	VODCĂ
WATER	APĂ
WHISKEY	WHISKY
WHITE WINE	VIN ALB

Review Jumble: The translations in the word list below have been scrambled. Draw lines between the left and right columns to find the correct translations.

```
N I N E C E Z E R P S I E R T S
H D O T T D L N O U Ă W C U S N
E C F I V E T N O I O D E N R N
C I E E V L E W T P D F Ş U I S
E N E E W X T A T L T K Ă B O C
Z C N T N E E T R U O F N Ă A E
E I N P N E E I T N S E T A Ă E
R S Ş A S R T I Ă S A Z E A O E
P P E Ş L H E O E P I H O O T T
S R H V Ş T Ş C A R E X A F H S
I E T A E E Ă U E E T D I I G D
O Z S D D N E R I Z V N R F I V
D E C A V S B T M E U T Ş T E A
L C W M I T A A O C E T Ş E U N
Ş E I P A I S P R E Z E C E M M
R N O L D Ă G Ş N Ă A D O N E Ş
```

ONE	DOISPREZECE
TWO	TREISPREZECE
THREE	UNU
FOUR	DOI
FIVE	ŞASE
SIX	NOUĂ
SEVEN	TREI
EIGHT	PATRU
NINE	ŞAPTE
TEN	CINCI
ELEVEN	ZECE
TWELVE	PAISPREZECE
THIRTEEN	UNSPREZECE
FOURTEEN	OPT
FIFTEEN	CINCISPREZECE

Review Time: Draw lines between the English word on the left and the corresponding translation on the right. Refer back to the original puzzle if you need help.

```
Ş Y E C E Z E R P S E T P A Ş Y
H A T N N O I L L I M B I I T T
N Ş P N O T T C O A O C P X Ş H
G E T T E V H P E S E M I A S G
M E E H E W T O E Z A S I S N I
O U K T I Z T V U N Ă Z Ş E O E
B P H A E R E R I S E U E V I V
S O T C E N T C E C A T O E L E
M N I S T A I Y I I H N R N I R
D W Ş E P A T N I G Z Ă D T M G
E C E Z E R P S I A Ş E O Y N F
R N Ă E O N E E T X I S C E U I
D N T F I C E Z I C N I C I O F
N Ş U D O U Ă Z E C I J A B A T
U L S U X R I C O C N I N E T Y
H N O U Ă S P R E Z E C E G T O
```

SIXTEEN	O SUTĂ
SEVENTEEN	UN MILION
EIGHTEEN	CINCIZECI
NINETEEN	ŞAPTESPREZECE
TWENTY	OPTZECI
THIRTY	PATRUZECI
FORTY	O MIE
FIFTY	DOUĂZECI
SIXTY	OPTSPREZECE
SEVENTY	TREIZECI
EIGHTY	NOUĂSPREZECE
NINETY	ŞAISPREZECE
HUNDRED	NOUĂZECI
THOUSAND	ŞAIZECI
MILLION	ŞAPTEZECI

Review Jumble: The translations in the word list below have been scrambled. Draw lines between the left and right columns to find the correct translations.

```
C A T I S T A S T Ă Z I T M R N
Ă Ă F W Y Ş D I Y C Ă V A Ă A A
W Ţ E Ă N A E A Z I I R T P G T
Y E S T E R D A Y N Ţ Ă A Q Â I
K R D F I S O S E I B Â O E O O
F A Ţ N E I S R R M Ş Â H J S N
I O Ţ U E Ş I Ă Â U O A L U F A
L T T Ă O S A S P D H W R W Â L
J Ă I S M Y D Y T T O T S E R H
D B L U N I A A Y W Ă A I E Ş O
E R E M E M E D Y H Â M N K I L
A Ă T O M O R R O W A Â Â E T I
Ţ S L W D N A U C T I I K N Ă D
E A E Ţ O D R T I U R N T D Ă A
W F R I D A Y A I O R E D Â Â Y
S U N D A Y U S D N A I Â E Ă L
```

MONDAY	DUMINICĂ
TUESDAY	SĂRBĂTOARE naţională
WEDNESDAY	SFÂRŞIT de săptămână
THURSDAY	JOI
FRIDAY	IERI
SATURDAY	SĂPTĂMÂNĂ
SUNDAY	MARŢI
WEEKEND	MÂINE
NATIONAL HOLIDAY	MIERCURI
TODAY	LUNI
TOMORROW	ASTĂZI
YESTERDAY	VINERI
WEEK	SÂMBĂTĂ
DAY	ZI

Review Time: Draw lines between the English
word on the left and the corresponding
translation on the right. Refer back to the
original puzzle if you need help.

```
T  J  O  W  H  U  N  L  I  R  P  A  V  D  N  I
J  U  L  Y  R  C  F  I  A  A  S  Q  G  P  Ă  J
T  N  H  I  A  M  R  D  L  O  T  S  U  G  U  A
K  E  I  R  A  U  N  A  I  U  L  I  E  Ă  N  N
L  A  O  R  D  E  C  E  M  B  R  I  E  E  S  U
N  G  T  R  L  R  E  O  T  C  L  T  I  A  E  A
O  I  N  A  T  E  G  Y  C  I  A  R  R  I  P  R
E  C  C  D  I  B  A  E  R  T  B  E  A  A  T  Y
P  O  R  N  R  M  I  P  Y  M  O  B  U  D  E  R
U  Ă  U  E  G  E  A  R  E  A  T  M  R  O  M  A
Y  I  I  L  B  V  A  I  E  D  O  E  B  H  B  U
N  U  I  A  U  O  O  U  E  R  O  C  E  R  R  R
A  E  O  C  H  N  T  S  G  T  S  E  F  A  I  B
V  E  E  A  N  R  Ă  C  N  U  R  D  E  H  E  E
A  U  D  T  I  H  T  N  O  M  S  Y  S  I  P  F
P  C  Q  X  N  A  R  E  B  M  E  T  P  E  S  E
```

JANUARY	OCTOMBRIE
FEBRUARY	FEBRUARIE
MARCH	NOIEMBRIE
APRIL	AUGUST
MAY	MAI
JUNE	LUNĂ
JULY	AN
AUGUST	IULIE
SEPTEMBER	DECEMBRIE
OCTOBER	IUNIE
NOVEMBER	CALENDAR
DECEMBER	IANUARIE
CALENDAR	SEPTEMBRIE
MONTH	MARTIE
YEAR	APRILIE

71

Review Jumble: The translations in the word list below have been scrambled. Draw lines between the left and right columns to find the correct translations.

```
T S E S Ă Ţ A E N I M I D A Ţ N
L O T U N I M A Ţ T O Y Z E B E
C A U E R R R H T H R M I N I G
C D N O C E S E C U N D Ă Y W O
V O I I M T T P T Ă I M V S I R
O D M M G T J N R H N A U C T Ă
Ă O U Y T H E E I I G M A T O R
Z S E M T C T D C W N A A M U O
A A T E N E D Ţ A E Ţ G H O Ţ A
I A P V C E E S E C O L H N T J
M D A Ă C O I C D M E Y E T U D
A R O E O S A A D Y I D C H Ă Ţ
Ă Ă N U L T Y S N H A A Ţ N K A
P I A A Ţ E S T T S W W R O F M
U Y F I A F T E R N O O N N E A
D L Ă R G A P R I M Ă V A R Ă A
```

WINTER	DIMINEAŢĂ
SPRING	PRIMĂVARĂ
SUMMER	SECOL
AUTUMN	DECENIU
SECOND	ORĂ
MINUTE	ZI
HOUR	SECUNDĂ
DAY	LUNĂ
MONTH	IARNĂ
YEAR	VARĂ
MORNING	NOAPTE
AFTERNOON	TOAMNĂ
NIGHT	MINUT
DECADE	AN
CENTURY	DUPĂ-AMIAZĂ

Review Time: Draw lines between the English word on the left and the corresponding translation on the right. Refer back to the original puzzle if you need help.

```
E N A E W I P A G S N E L O E T
T M O E A F B O Ş T T T T R E N
O M S E O A E N L O E Ş T D A A
U R Ş O V C O U K F T N D S G Ş
R T V K A Y S I H Ş A D R A D T
T G V H D L B D K B D A H R A T
S Ş E Z U G L M C Y N I T W P W
A T E I O U A P A E T I N A R I
B W R D E R S L L R R O Ş U H N
L U O E R G O S B G O W I T I M
A D C L D E E I O E H T I B B V
F E C X L N V L V I N U R I I I
K N I P Y E D V T I R O M O N L
T G R E E N Y E G O W G L E E D
E U L B L I O R A N G E A N E S
P O R T O C A L I U T N A Ş T Ş
```

BLACK	VIOLET
BLUE	PORTOCALIU
BROWN	ROZ
GOLD	ALB
GREY	ALBASTRU
GREEN	VERDE
ORANGE	MARO
PINK	GRI
PURPLE	ROŞU
RED	NEGRU
SILVER	AURIU
WHITE	ARGINTIU
YELLOW	GALBEN

Review Jumble: The translations in the word list below have been scrambled. Draw lines between the left and right columns to find the correct translations.

```
S E L S H O R F I B M F T F G I
Q D C E R E H P S F E R Ă N N O
U P I L V A E B C B A T M E A E
A R E G I S E O U I J R L S A O
R E D N I L Y C V C L C I R D E
E C F A T Ă D I M A R I P H I I
L T T I A A Q H T I L H N I M H
N A W R D A G N C O I G A D A G
N N N T Ă I O O V A L N Ă I R N
G G T N O G A T N E P U S A Y U
H L N A O R E M S T H I C M P T
E E O T R G M T O A E R A A L P
A T C O C T A G O N E T R N E E
T O O F T R Ă X P C D T B T S R
J P N O P E O P E L C T S E G D
N Ă E F C H E T E H E X A G O N
```

CIRCLE	CILINDRU
CONE	PIRAMIDĂ
CUBE	PENTAGON
CYLINDER	TRIUNGHI
DIAMOND	HEXAGON
HEXAGON	CUB
OCTAGON	OVAL
OVAL	DREPTUNGHI
PENTAGON	CERC
PYRAMID	OCTOGON
RECTANGLE	PĂTRAT
SPHERE	SFERĂ
SQUARE	STEA
STAR	CON
TRIANGLE	DIAMANT

Review Time: Draw lines between the English word on the left and the corresponding translation on the right. Refer back to the original puzzle if you need help.

```
Ț Ă Ț A F Ț D D N D E C F T E G
X B H L C Ă Y P F P H O S E Y E
O M Â A F A Â S W O R B E Y E S
L I P S B Ă R B I E B A I U L N
Ț L Ț D S T E Â H H O R G F A O
Â A A N C U R E C H E N A Â S T
S E E H I H A S O N O C O Z H T
H N E B Ă D I O R T E Z E T E Y
I E T N U R F N J I H W U E S S
K C A C E Z U O I E A O T P T N
N N O R T G E G S L M H A Â Ț E
S Â A R U F A E L D A R O O S Â
Ă R Ă S Ț D R C X R D Ă O R S I
W P T U T T S E T H E A H D T D
N S E R Z C H E B I C Ț S Â S I
S L D H D S Y E G N B D T H O A
```

CHEEK	PĂR
CHIN	SPRÂNCENE
EAR	OBRAZ
EYE	OCHI
EYEBROWS	DINȚI
EYELASHES	NAS
FACE	GURĂ
FOREHEAD	BUZE
HAIR	GENE
HEAD	CAP
LIPS	LIMBĂ
MOUTH	FAȚĂ
NOSE	URECHE
TEETH	BĂRBIE
TONGUE	FRUNTE

Review Jumble: The translations in the word list below have been scrambled. Draw lines between the left and right columns to find the correct translations.

```
L X N Ş E N E Ţ P Q L O N V V D
I E K R Ă E I D A T R U W E H E
F T B G R I L I H R O O O S L G
Â Î R C A Â Î P I E B G O F F E
G T A R O I C I P L E F P V Ă T
S O M Â Ă R U T E I E H C N Î D
O X E F D M E Ă A R N Y O E Ş E
A L Ţ S N L U T A L I E T S W L
I E X T A E O M A Ă P Î H R A A
X Â L I H G L Ş N N R O I C I P
T D R S A U Â Â Ă M U S M H S I
Î O E O T L M Ă O L T E R O T C
T R O E E E U B D H Ş H E S A I
N F G F I N G E R W O A Î X H O
N E D A L B R E D L U O H S A R
D G D E Ă Ă Â E D H Î E T D T Î
```

ARM	BRAŢ
ELBOW	UMĂR
FINGER	OMOPLAT
FOOT	DEGET DE LA PICIOR
HAND	SFÂRC
HIP	MÂNĂ
LEG	DEGETUL MARE
NIPPLE	ŞOLD
SHOULDER	COT
SHOULDER BLADE	PICIOR
THUMB	ÎNCHEIETURĂ
TOE	PICIOR
WAIST	DEGET
WRIST	TALIE

Review Time: Draw lines between the English word on the left and the corresponding translation on the right. Refer back to the original puzzle if you need help.

```
D I H W Y N W T T O R T R T F Â
T Q N A I D H G K C A B R F Ț R
S A C M T T L E T N Ț W L Y S F
E K T A R E P F K B E T T Ț N B
L D I A Z A S L S N U R A Â E W
I H C N U N E G T L D E S H D C
A E Ă T S A E R B Ț Ă D E Â D G
N A I E P V T O O J Â S Ă E H T
R C E B A E E B N F Â S A Ă N S
E Ă O R T L L F T Ă Â E N E C K
G T W A E T E L T B Â F P R O C
N T H Ț P S I I D M L C R G O O
I R H I E S P Y H A S S I O Â T
F V Ț M G M Ă D C G Â T P R E T
N T A O R H T O E N N L T M U U
L Ă R A O U S B U S P U E J E B
```

ANKLE	SUBSUOARĂ
ARMPIT	GENUNCHI
BACK	GÂT
BODY	ANTEBRAȚ
BREAST	GAMBĂ
BUTTOCKS	PIELE
CALF	GLEZNĂ
FINGERNAIL	COAPSĂ
FOREARM	SPATE
KNEE	BURIC
NAVEL	SÂN
NECK	FESE
SKIN	CORP
THIGH	GÂT
THROAT	UNGHIE

Review Jumble: The translations in the word list below have been scrambled. Draw lines between the left and right columns to find the correct translations.

```
L R S Ț Ă N R N A P E N D I C E
A H C A M O T S I A E Ă T O N N
R P Ș R N Ă H H R R N H T E H I
G E P T Z Ș C E R T R E V O Y T
E Ă S E Â I V Ă A E R I Ț B U S
I A N R N I E C T R I S U Â A E
N O O I L D I Ă Y E T E G E Ă T
T Y R E L F I E M O O D R N O N
E E V S F P E X M I E C M C U I
S N E G N Â S A I Â N U S M X L
T D I P A N C R E A S I U B L L
I I N Â M Ă L P P C R Ș R Â O A
N K S S D D O O L B C A M T Ț M
E X M S P L E E N H I D Ș G T S
L E I N T E S T I N U L G R O S
T H Ț D I Ț O T E U Z Z M Ș S T
```

APPENDIX	PLĂMÂNII
ARTERIES	INTESTINUL GROS
BLOOD	STOMAC
BRAIN	intestinul SUBȚIRE
HEART	PANCREAS
KIDNEY	SÂNGE
LARGE INTESTINE	CREIER
LIVER	FICAT
LUNGS	INIMĂ
MUSCLES	MUȘCHI
PANCREAS	ARTERE
SMALL INTESTINE	SPLINĂ
SPLEEN	APENDICE
STOMACH	RINICHI
VEINS	VENE

Review Time: Draw lines between the English word on the left and the corresponding translation on the right. Refer back to the original puzzle if you need help.

```
A F R I C A Y E W L U N A E C O
O H R A S V E N I D U T I T A L
E C H N K O I D R R L P N T N T
L T E T O A U O U A A A T A O A
O H C A E R N T N T E E P S R N
N E U R N E T T H C I O H I T T
G D A C D U I H O A R G E A H A
I U T T Q C L C A U M L N C P R
T T O I O O I P E M O E O O O C
U I R C E F O P A P E N R T L T
D T E A I L O F H C T R A I E I
I A A C U R R T E I I U I I C C
N L A L U I U E N R Q F E C S A
E P S E C O H E S E Z I I R A A
L U Y A S T N E N I T N O C D B
D U S E D T D R O N L U L O P R
```

AFRICA	EUROPA
ANTARCTICA	CONTINENT
ASIA	ASIA
ATLANTIC OCEAN	america DE NORD
CONTINENT	LATITUDINE
EQUATOR	POLUL NORD
EUROPE	OCEANUL atlantic
LATITUDE	america DE SUD
LONGITUDE	AFRICA
NORTH AMERICA	POLUL SUD
NORTH POLE	OCEANUL PACIFIC
PACIFIC OCEAN	LONGITUDINE
SOUTH AMERICA	ECUATOR
SOUTH POLE	ANTARCTICA

Review Jumble: The translations in the word list below have been scrambled. Draw lines between the left and right columns to find the correct translations.

```
A E F E E R L A R O C H E N G O
O B H R E C I F D E C O R A L I
E A E U E W G E D T S A O C A S
R A C D M T S N E F Ş Ş P L C O
A A A Ă O E A E O S U L S U I F
M O A P R L M R A N A R I V E R
O F H T S U E E C J A Ă L L R S
U N C I N S U L Ă O C E A N W Ş
N I A T T R X A C Ţ A K C C Ş Ş
T R E C Ş E D Ş I R E S T O S A
A E B F L A G D T Ă A W T Ş S Y
I Ţ L E Ş O Ş E Y K I T R Ă E P
N Ş S N R A V H T A E A E Â X Ş
S W L A F Z I R T S H S Ş R U Â
Ţ R Ş A F F E E F A G H E Ţ A R
F G T N H E O U S E B Y D T T S
```

BEACH	RÂU
CITY	MARE
COAST	PĂDURE
CORAL REEF	MUNTE
CRATER	INSULĂ
DESERT	RECIF DE CORALI
FOREST	LAC
GLACIER	COASTĂ
ISLAND	DEŞERT
LAKE	VULCAN
MOUNTAIN	GHEŢAR
OCEAN	ORAŞ
RIVER	PLAJĂ
SEA	CRATER
VOLCANO	OCEAN

Review Time: Draw lines between the English word on the left and the corresponding translation on the right. Refer back to the original puzzle if you need help.

```
C L N S D H U R R I C A N E D A
I I O N H T Ă E H H D H T U N E
R G I O I I C O T H U N D E R M
T H O W W E T L N N I M E O O U
E T L F O T L I O B E N I A A K
M N Z U E B U C R U C O L D Î Q
O I Ă G R U N E O O D E R N S N
R N P C M E I I S W S Y A E N Ă
A G A E V F X P A A U N T Ț V Y
B L D G F U L G E R N U Î S Ă S
D I Ă T A O A Î K M N Ț Y M N I
Î H R F A R R O T E Y L T C Ă T
B T Ă I I R U A T O G H R Z T E
Ă S E C E C U I I M I N S Ă O T
T E O P R E S I U N E Ă W A Ț G
S T G Î R Ț A E E L Q D Ă T R T
```

BAROMETRIC pressure	URAGAN
CLOUDY	FULGER
COLD	ÎNSORIT
FOG	ZĂPADĂ
HOT	RECE
HUMID	PRESIUNE barometrică
HURRICANE	CALD
LIGHTNING	TUNET
RAIN	CEAȚĂ
RAINBOW	NOROS
SNOW	FIERBINTE
SUNNY	CURCUBEU
THUNDER	PLOAIE
WARM	UMED

Review Jumble: The translations in the word list below have been scrambled. Draw lines between the left and right columns to find the correct translations.

```
H D O S T R I C H Y E N A V F R
E Z D L N E C H I M P A N Z E E
S W E N G Ţ I E H D R L H H O C
R U Ă B A R B E Z E A I N Ţ L O
W S S T R U Ţ T S N P O I W L N
T U O O O Ă Y A N O E N U X Ă I
R M E R A E P H P O E M B F Y R
L A E Z E N E O L E O P A R D D
N T O O N C T E L Ţ F R B Ă H R
R O V C Ţ A O E T I I F N E A A
V P O C M P P N L G T E A L Ă P
Ţ O O B A H A M I O I N L R L E
E P S R A F O S I H P I A Y I H
Ă P D N E B O W X C R E T D R G
I I T L E Ă N E N O R N S T O O
S H E A R M B R G D E A T S G O
```

ANTELOPE	ZEBRĂ
BABOON	GORILĂ
CHEETAH	BABUIN
CHIMPANZEE	GHEPARD
ELEPHANT	CIMPANZEU
GIRAFFE	HIENĂ
GORILLA	ANTILOPĂ
HIPPOPOTAMUS	RINOCER
HYENA	GIRAFĂ
LEOPARD	LEU
LION	STRUŢ
OSTRICH	HIPOPOTAM
RHINOCEROS	LEOPARD
ZEBRA	ELEFANT

Review Time: Draw lines between the English word on the left and the corresponding translation on the right. Refer back to the original puzzle if you need help.

```
L U I N Ş U R S P O L A R O U Ş
T K I Ş D J P I S I C Ă S N E W
T R T E G O I W L A H Â A S Ă W
O T E D P T O I N E E I G A M Ş
I N N S C L A G Ă E T M Ă J G J
T Z C O F C U C N C N T T A A O
Ş A L T C R U V A N A D O G P Ş
I Ă U Ă M E V T L N Ă T U U O N
E E H D Ă S Ă D E G I A Â A L I
I E C Ş E Ă T T S Ă R U R R A U
I N I T L E L T U U E E G K R G
A E N I Â C T I O L C L U N B N
A S H G F E L B M E E R U P E I
F O X E A E R B T Ă G M U M A P
M O O R A G N A K I C L A I R E
Ş M F Â Ş T B R T H R R T C S E
```

BAT	TIGRU
CAMEL	CÂINE
CAT	LILIAC
DOG	ELAN
FOX	CĂMILĂ
JAGUAR	URS POLAR
KANGAROO	PINGUIN
MOOSE	ŞOARECE
MOUSE	PISICĂ
MULE	JAGUAR
PENGUIN	LUP
POLAR BEAR	CANGUR
RABBIT	VULPE
TIGER	CATÂR
WOLF	IEPURE

Review Jumble: The translations in the word list below have been scrambled. Draw lines between the left and right columns to find the correct translations.

```
Ţ H I E D R G M U H T Ş G M E Ţ
K F O Ă U H O O Ş T V O C N R Ţ
V N M S N M T I Ţ N R E V A E B
Ş V U C T Ă M Ă L F P G C T E T
N S S K A U M I N O L C B U L H
A O O S S S D A A E O W R G I A
L N P S Q O T R L O K G O N D P
O I O C C U A O N S E O A A O B
B P L O G Ţ I Ş R N Ş G S R C L
O S R N O T A R S A Ş Ă C U O A
Ş C A C F H H R R K Ş U Ă Q R C
D R Ş S E I U P I E P B M A C K
O O A N H U E Ş L I L L A M A B
H P O T H Ă Ţ I N F U B E H U E
I U N Ă Ţ I R E V E V C E Ţ E A
T S Ţ S E A W T S W R A Y H T R
```

BEAVER	OPOSUM
BLACK BEAR	LAMĂ
CROCODILE	ŞOBOLAN
FROG	BUFNIŢĂ
LLAMA	RATON
OPOSSUM	URS NEGRU
ORANGUTAN	CASTOR
OWL	PORC SPINOS
PORCUPINE	CROCODIL
RACCOON	BROASCĂ
RAT	ŞARPE
SKUNK	URANGUTAN
SNAKE	VEVERIŢĂ
SQUIRREL	SCONCS

Review Time: Draw lines between the English word on the left and the corresponding translation on the right. Refer back to the original puzzle if you need help.

```
I Y Ş F G C E W B A R C M H Ţ E
R A M A L A C M S A Ă E E L E A
H S I F Y L L E J Ţ L Ă E A A P
O A I O U W M N I W C E L A H W
M O Ă R C N M T O O S C N L U Ă
A T S L S T A R F I S H I Ă Ă E
R S U O S C O H T Ă L E F S T T
Ş E R E A T O P S G Z A L Ş I V
T T L R N P S Q U I D U E I A X
T A A A N T S H C S F P D S D H
L C W M N I H C E R T G H E S M
I S N E O O H E I U A A D E M G
O A E D I R V P R H R B A I M J
F O C U Q C S T L K I L O C T V
L R I E Ţ Ă L Ă L O B S T E R O
H B E L D E R A M E D A E T S O
```

TURTLE   HOMAR
CRAB   ORCĂ
DOLPHIN   MORSĂ
FISH   DELFIN
JELLYFISH   MEDUZĂ
LOBSTER   STEA DE MARE
OCTOPUS   CALAMAR
ORCA   BALENĂ
SEA LION   PEŞTE
SEAL   LEU DE MARE
SHARK   FOCĂ
SQUID   BROASCA TESTOASA
STARFISH   CARACATIŢĂ
WALRUS   CRAB
WHALE   RECHIN

Review Jumble: The translations in the word list below have been scrambled. Draw lines between the left and right columns to find the correct translations.

```
F R A D P I U O U B N O I F O U
F I I C Ă Ş U T Ă M U B A S C L
H R Y U R M T O P E N N A E A H
K E L U I F A I C R C G I R D S
Ă H I O N H E M O T H E R C S E
C T M L Ţ A S O N E I E Q D Q G
I O A U I T T U N R H R S Ă R R
N M F O N M A P E T A R F Ş E A
U D B E P E A S A A W S T L T N
B N R C N E P F T E C Ţ C O H D
H A O E O T N H K R E N O S G F
P R T I P P A N E E U T A Ţ U A
L G H N S Ţ I T H W C A W D A T
Ă I E O R H S I Ă G S E M D D H
N E R D L I H C W V Ş Ţ I S A E
H Ă D D S O H L O T I M F N O R
```

AUNT	UNCHI
BROTHER	FRATE
CHILDREN	SORĂ
DAUGHTER	FIICĂ
FAMILY	FAMILIE
FATHER	MĂTUŞĂ
GRANDFATHER	FIU
GRANDMOTHER	NEPOATĂ
MOTHER	COPII
NEPHEW	TATĂ
NIECE	PĂRINŢI
PARENTS	NEPOT
SISTER	MAMĂ
SON	BUNICĂ
UNCLE	BUNIC

Review Time: Draw lines between the English word on the left and the corresponding translation on the right. Refer back to the original puzzle if you need help.

```
M P B A D Y E R T I E Ţ A Ş E E
F W A L N I N O S A S E M Ă N T
A A B F Ţ Ă Ă H K O N N G N R O
T L Y O Ă T A N M U C M F H H A
H N S R A A T L Ă M Y R U Ş S R
E I N O M F Ă R C A O S U C I Z
R R P Ş E O O I G N B L O R X I
I E T I O N T G I A E W S C H W
N H Ţ R E I Ă H N B Ş P O E P T
L T Ă E T O M D E O Ă U O S U T
A O L V N W C B R R S I T T O F
W R E D Ţ Ţ I A E I I D A R Ş U
A B E T H O W F N S E N N T T P
U U A N S I S T E R I N L A W Ş
G D Ş R E T H G U A D D N A R G
P A D A U G H T E R I N L A W G
```

BROTHER-IN-LAW	SOŢIE
BABY	FATĂ
BOY	NEPOATĂ
COUSIN	BĂIAT
DAUGHTER-IN-LAW	BEBELUŞ
FATHER-IN-LAW	NEPOT
GIRL	CUMNAT
GRANDDAUGHTER	NORĂ
GRANDSON	SOŢ
HUSBAND	SOACRĂ
MOTHER-IN-LAW	VERIŞOR
SISTER-IN-LAW	GINERE
SON-IN-LAW	SOCRU
WIFE	CUMNATĂ

Review Jumble: The translations in the word list below have been scrambled. Draw lines between the left and right columns to find the correct translations.

```
U C S C H N K T I K R J H Y M N
I L Î T K N O A D Z F P H E Â F
T N P Ă I A I A M R U A A T A A
A Ş O H H M A T N Â C A O Ş Â O
A T T Â R O I O Ă P N S A G N A
Â O Ş O F A Z R E L E C D Ş W T
T C D E W G T E A E P E A E O T
P A T O T O P A Y E H A L C L A
P R T A G Â N D I A H Â O S L Î
A R O P E A P E A A G O H A O N
K Y S Ă E O H N V R K I T D F T
N M I E O T T I E T U E T Ă O R
S O N I O I Ş H D H S X A Ă T E
F H G A C Ă R A E B O T F Y G B
L A S C H I M B A C I T I E Y A
G K I Ă S T D A E G N A H C O T
```

TO ASK	A CÂNTA
TO BE	A VEDEA
TO CARRY	A FI
TO CHANGE	A CITI
TO COOK	A SCHIMBA
TO EAT	A ÎNTREBA
TO FOLLOW	A GÂNDI
TO HEAR	A PLĂTI
TO PAY	A GĂTI
TO READ	A MÂNCA
TO SEE	A CĂRA
TO SING	A DORMI
TO SLEEP	A AŞTEPTA
TO THINK	A URMA
TO WAIT	A AUZI

Review Time: Draw lines between the English word on the left and the corresponding translation on the right. Refer back to the original puzzle if you need help.

```
H V R A C Ă L Ă T O R I R F Ă D
R F E G E L E Ţ N Î A S O O A N
R M V M S I V I E D I H C N Î A
I I A B O V A O A V I N D E H T
X H H D L E R I K R O W O T A S
V E O H C T T T U R I L B Î T R
Ţ T T A O A O O V B I U O A I E
E R F H T F T S D A I A T T B D
A A E U I H O E P R E B T U C N
Y L J N N T C L E E I V Î Ă A U
P A D Ţ E I O L A T A N A C N O
A E V Ă V H M T O L D K K A M T
Ă E Ţ O A T E R A M U N C I Î Ţ
Ă Î N E R A O O E K Ă A O I X Ă
S I H A E B A H D E E Î E Y N O
D E A G Ă S I T O L O O K F O R
```

TO CLOSE	A MUNCI
TO COME	A BEA
TO DO	A CĂUTA
TO DRINK	A ÎNCHIDE
TO FIND	A AVEA
TO HAVE	A IUBI
TO HELP	A LUA
TO LOOK FOR	A VINDE
TO LOVE	A VENI
TO SELL	A AJUTA
TO SPEAK	A ÎNŢELEGE
TO TAKE	A VORBI
TO TRAVEL	A CĂLĂTORI
TO UNDERSTAND	A GĂSI
TO WORK	A FACE

Review Jumble: The translations in the word list below have been scrambled. Draw lines between the left and right columns to find the correct translations.

```
E T O D A N C E E D L G Y E H Ţ
H O O Ţ V P A R Ă P M U C A O H
Ă O Q L R M A K T E B L E Ş T O
D W O Ş E I L Ş T O K N O W E T
E E Ş R A A E I T Ă O A Î S I D
L R G H W R R O Ş I Y P S J D L
S E R O Ş W G N L M Î I E Î H M
Ţ Î T H O O A E T E Ş Z E N O E
U R C T Î O O G Y N I E V N A M
Ă W J Y O E R R L A A E I U M A
B A S T N L A E L S R W G R Ă S
O E I E O P E M T E A O O O Ş C
O N S I L P S A C S Ş E T T Ţ R
R S S E Ţ E L D V A U N R A B I
L A C U J E S A D E S C H I D E
I A S N A D A R Y A Ţ Ă V N Î A
```

TO BUY	A DESCHIDE
TO DANCE	A SCRIE
TO GIVE	A ŞTI
TO GO	A DATORA
TO KNOW	A DA
TO LEARN	A MERGE
TO LEAVE	A SE JUCA
TO OPEN	A MERGE
TO OWE	A ÎNVĂŢA
TO PLAY	A PLECA
TO RUN	A DANSA
TO WALK	A ALERGA
TO WANT	A VREA
TO WRITE	A CUMPĂRA

Review Time: Draw lines between the English word on the left and the corresponding translation on the right. Refer back to the original puzzle if you need help.

```
E T A L O C O H C A G S W R H T
I C E S E N I Â P N G C T E G T
H I R N Y G N X C I U S L E O W
L O R F L O U R C L F F G I R S
T C U R F S S M U L B Ă T Ă Ă U
S O T U T E N I E R B O M E P G
D L C I A Â B L S X M H W H S A
Â A L T W Â C K I M B U T T E R
R T E U O L I G E O R N S G L I
O Ă D R S A L A D C G T G Ă B U
E D H W B A T H L F H S S R A A
E T S A P X L W A Ă O E Â I T T
T O R E Z E U A P I U N E S E C
P A D I T T Â T T N Z O A S G E
E S E I C Â L E E Ă L P Â S E H
Y Ă H Ă G E N R A C Ă O U E V E
```

BREAD	APĂ
BUTTER	ZAHĂR
CHEESE	BRÂNZĂ
CHOCOLATE	PASTE
EGGS	OUĂ
FLOUR	LEGUME
FRUIT	PÂINE
MEAT	FRUCT
MILK	CIOCOLATĂ
PASTA	UNT
RICE	FĂINĂ
SALAD	LAPTE
SUGAR	SALATĂ
VEGETABLES	CARNE
WATER	OREZ

Review Jumble: The translations in the word list below have been scrambled. Draw lines between the left and right columns to find the correct translations.

```
A O T U E N I W Y H H B P G N P
O O Ă Ț S A D R A M N E G U U N
C Ț W S A L T R U A I R L I O C
D S A R Y O G U R T B E E F E A
H N S R K S A N S B I M R S Ă R
R D O Q Î F T F S O I J A E C N
Y A E Î O C B R O E U R Ă L R E
Y Ț M U U H A L L S E P R R O D
H I O A B E I K C U I N S S P E
N E T Ă R E M P E P P E R Ă E V
E L G S S V E D E Ă I K A W D I
O R D Ă Y T V R E K R C E Î E T
T G L Î N E I L O O T I T T N Ă
U O U H O N N O P V H H O I R E
T U I B M N C O I C E C R E A M
F S O L N Î N G H E Ț A T Ă C R
```

BEEF	PIPER
BEER	IAURT
CAKE	CARNE DE PORC
CHICKEN	SUPĂ
COOKIES	PUI
HONEY	CARNE DE VITĂ
ICE CREAM	ÎNGHEȚATĂ
LAMB	ULEI
OIL	VIN
PEPPER	TORT
PORK	MIEL
SALT	BERE
SOUP	MIERE
WINE	SARE
YOGURT	PRĂJITURI

Review Time: Draw lines between the English
word on the left and the corresponding
translation on the right. Refer back to the
original puzzle if you need help.

```
O T T C S E I R R E B W A R T S
G A U P I I N U Ş P Ă C G T N Y
S Ă S N E Ă P Ă Ă C H R A V L R
Y M A D T P I I I N E S Â I N T
H A N B P H E S N P I N H E S R
V N A I R O R N F E Ă F C I B Ă
M H N O L E M R E T A W A Â L D
W U A G I D U E Ă I I P E M U H
N N L P A T Ş B G U O I P Ă E D
O P E P E N E V E R D E N L B O
A E G G P L A N T F A U P I E T
I W T T T Z N O E E R N I A R A
N E S T T O C I R P A T A A R U
R Ă I Ă M A D O R A N G E T I Ă
R Ş M E L O N T G R A P E S E C
O E L Ă R H I R U G U R T S S Ş
```

APRICOT	VÂNĂTĂ
BLUEBERRIES	PEPENE
EGGPLANT	STRUGURI
GRAPEFRUIT	AFINĂ
GRAPES	PIERSICĂ
LEMON	CAISĂ
MELON	GREPFRUT
ORANGE	CĂPŞUNI
PEACH	PARĂ
PEAR	RODIE
PINEAPPLE	PORTOCALĂ
PLUM	PRUNĂ
POMEGRANATE	LĂMÂIE
STRAWBERRIES	ANANAS
WATERMELON	PEPENE VERDE

Review Jumble: The translations in the word list below have been scrambled. Draw lines between the left and right columns to find the correct translations.

```
R L C N E B L A G E N E P E P T
E E I Â A S S E I R R E H C T Ş
Y C P M A R D E I R O Ş U A T Î
E E T U E I D H W I S A I N Ş A
L L L Ă M Â I E V E R D E T N N
L V G A P P L E I D Ă D O A E S
O O I R S Ă K R E G M M N L M Ş
W D F Ş E X R I E Ş A A N O B I
P O P Ş Â E V I N T B L C U A Ă
E V S X B E N U O C E H B P N R
P L W P R I S P R A I E T E A U
P E S D H Q Â T E N E R I C N E
E A E C U E N D Ă P C E E Ş Ă M
R C C A E L V O D W P M S Ş O Z
U U S F A M U R E D P E P P E R
Z H N T B L A C K B E R R I E S
```

APPLE	BANANĂ
BANANA	MURE
BLACKBERRIES	ARDEI GALBEN
CANTALOUPE	DOVLEAC
CHERRIES	ZMEURĂ
FIG	ROŞIE
GREEN PEPPER	MĂR
LIME	SMOCHINĂ
PUMPKIN	PEPENE GALBEN
RASPBERRIES	LĂMÂIE VERDE
RED PEPPER	CIREŞE
SQUASH	ARDEI VERDE
TOMATO	ARDEI ROŞU
YELLOW PEPPER	DOVLECEL
ZUCCHINI	DOVLEAC

Review Time: Draw lines between the English
word on the left and the corresponding
translation on the right. Refer back to the
original puzzle if you need help.

```
T S T E E B G W U S T U R O I E
S S P E D R E V E R Ă Z A M E T
E T D I G A A O Ă C A R T O F I
D C Ă O N A T N L E T T U C E A
R A O C N A B C I I C I L R A G
E U N N T I C B C H Ă E W S U T
V L E O O A N H A E G J L A V S
Ă I P E H P O Ț A C A N S E A N
T F I Y T K I L R M C P A P R D
A L E L E L N D V O A Ă Ă N Z Y
L O A I O E O R Ă R R E R E Ă Ț
A W O C E C E L A C R T R E M E
S E O Y N A C G C O O F H R K L
S R A S H E U O S V T E E G A I
B E T O F S P A R A N G H E L N
T O T S P A N A C B R K A L E Ă
```

ARTICHOKE	SPARANGHEL
ASPARAGUS	MORCOV
BEETS	BROCOLI
BROCCOLI	VARZĂ
CABBAGE	CONOPIDĂ
CARROT	SFECLĂ
CAULIFLOWER	CEAPĂ
CELERY	SALATĂ VERDE
GARLIC	KALE
GREEN PEAS	SPANAC
KALE	MAZĂRE VERDE
LETTUCE	USTUROI
ONION	ȚELINĂ
POTATOES	CARTOFI
SPINACH	ANGHINARE

Review Jumble: The translations in the word list below have been scrambled. Draw lines between the left and right columns to find the correct translations.

```
E  S  G  E  N  E  W  X  E  E  N  Ş  R  I  A  A
S  U  F  R  A  G  E  R  I  E  G  O  A  Ş  M  L
E  I  R  Ă  T  Ă  C  U  B  A  T  H  R  O  O  M
M  S  T  L  N  S  E  S  R  I  W  G  O  S  O  C
E  Ă  U  D  R  A  G  A  M  R  T  O  B  E  R  E
D  L  R  O  A  C  J  R  Q  T  N  U  D  O  G  E
Ă  Ş  P  T  H  C  O  M  N  T  S  Y  E  N  N  T
L  A  I  A  S  D  B  E  Ă  T  E  N  B  I  I  H
A  P  A  R  T  A  M  E  N  T  G  S  E  A  V  W
S  O  S  E  E  T  E  E  D  E  P  K  T  M  I  I
S  H  S  G  R  P  M  R  E  R  I  L  L  N  L  E
A  Ş  R  A  A  E  O  E  E  T  O  A  L  H  S  H
E  D  P  R  S  A  F  C  C  F  W  O  F  N  L  N
U  A  G  A  Z  O  N  H  A  N  R  N  M  W  T  M
H  O  B  G  O  G  E  N  Ă  Ş  E  E  I  Ă  G  I
M  O  O  R  G  N  I  N  I  D  X  F  C  O  I  Ş
```

APARTMENT	CASĂ
BASEMENT	SUFRAGERIE
BATHROOM	GARAJ
BED	SUBSOL
BEDROOM	DORMITOR
DINING ROOM	FEREASTRĂ
FENCE	PAT
GARAGE	GARD
HOUSE	ACOPERIŞ
KITCHEN	BAIE
LAWN	GAZON
LIVING ROOM	SALĂ DE MESE
ROOF	APARTAMENT
WINDOW	BUCĂTĂRIE

Review Time: Draw lines between the English word on the left and the corresponding translation on the right. Refer back to the original puzzle if you need help.

```
O O M A Ş I N Ă D E S P Ă L A T
O C T P A L U D Ş B E H O S Q Ă
A O S Ă E T A C N I A T R U C I
Ş V L C T R O T A R I P S A C E
C O Ă A L E D S T D S C Ă R I U
N R S N M O L E D E Ă T S H R H
A F T D I P O A A T N O U E E Ă
I I A E H C Ă P O H G I I A S H
Ş R I L C E S R G T R L B A S T
E E R A A U D I W N E E M O E A
M P S B D E A A P D I T Y P R B
I L Ă R R I A F N R A M R R D L
N A B U T H T A B E L A M P D E
E C F Z O H H M U U C A V I Ş Ă
U E N I H C A M G N I H S A W I
T M N R I D T K O Y D P O G Y S
```

BATHTUB	MAŞINĂ DE SPĂLAT
CARPET	PISCINĂ
CHANDELIER	USCĂTOR DE RUFE
CURTAIN	PERDEA
DRESSER	SCĂRI
DRYER	CADĂ
FAUCET	MASĂ
FIREPLACE	TOALETĂ
LAMP	ROBINET
SWIMMING POOL	ASPIRATOR
STAIRS	ŞEMINEU
TABLE	DULAP
TOILET	COVOR
VACUUM	CANDELABRU
WASHING MACHINE	LAMPĂ

Review Jumble: The translations in the word list below have been scrambled. Draw lines between the left and right columns to find the correct translations.

```
U Ț Q Ă Ț E A T Ă I F P T R R T
U T B D U E C Ă N R E P E C E O
Y P I Ă Ș S K Y N T I H B R F R
E A C L O S E T D L S A U Ă R H
R L D V E N T I L A T O R R I H
Ț I S D M S Ș O W O R N N O G H
D P H I Ă G W H I I H D U Ș E I
P O H A M D S E B Ț C H A I R D
A C E I L I N G F A N F C S A N
L E H S D L M I R R O R S S T E
U D T I C A W W L C R I B E O S
D Ț K L U U Y A B G Ă G R R R H
Ț U N O A V P H Y O O I O T A O
Ț T I Ș Ț S E T O F V D Ă T T W
F Ă S P Ă L Ă T O R D E V A S E
Ț P Z E R E L G Ă R N R N M I R
```

CHAIR	HORN
CEILING FAN	PERNĂ
CHIMNEY	CUPTOR
CLOSET	SPĂLĂTOR DE VASE
CRIB	SALTEA
DESK	VENTILATOR
DISHWASHER	CHIUVETĂ
HALLWAY	SCAUN
MATTRESS	OGLINDĂ
MIRROR	FRIGIDER
OVEN	PĂTUȚ DE COPIL
PILLOW	BIROU
REFRIGERATOR	HOL
SHOWER	DULAP
SINK	DUȘ

Review Time: Draw lines between the English word on the left and the corresponding translation on the right. Refer back to the original puzzle if you need help.

```
E H Ă N O O P S E L B A T Y J Ţ
F S O N S S A L G E N I W I O U
T H S Ş A I H Ţ E S S A L G Ă R
L E Ă L R C A S T R O N P E H N
T Y D I F A R F U R I E U K H E
H I Ţ N E Ş D Ţ O S S E F H I Y
T F Ţ G A T E A S P O O N I M N
O A U U Ş L V R O T R S R N N E
L Ţ A R C I I O V O I E M I N K
C Ă O I C L N N I E H C T A S R
E D P Ţ G U M C G C Ţ B L A A O
L E E Ă K R L O T U E E M Ă L F
B M P A E U P I P E R Ş L Y T P
A A P T L N P I Ţ A E Ă W Ă L T
T S E D T S H E S Ă O G O Ţ O N
A Ă R U G N I L Ă O I H B T O M
```

BOWL	ULCIOR
FORK	FAŢĂ DE MASĂ
GLASS	FURCULIŢĂ
KNIFE	FARFURIE
MUG	LINGURĂ
NAPKIN	ŞERVEŢEL
PEPPER	PIPER
PITCHER	LINGURIŢĂ
PLATE	LINGURĂ
SALT	PAHAR DE VIN
SPOON	STICLĂ
TABLECLOTH	CANĂ
TABLESPOON	SARE
TEASPOON	CASTRON
WINE GLASS	CUŢIT

Review Jumble: The translations in the word list below have been scrambled. Draw lines between the left and right columns to find the correct translations.

```
T A R U S Ă M E D Ă T E L U R A
Ă J S Ă U Ţ T E T P Ţ D U E P J
Z W C R E I O N H Ș S I S O E U
E E A T N N H A M M E R L E N M
C A T S F L T G W N E L G U C O
N F N Ă O E I N R I O B C I I S
A E C R F B A F L U U Ă O L L P
R C E E B U Ș P P A B C E L I E
F A N I U R O P I I A V D M T I
E N D F R U T T A N E R N K W P
I B U R U Ș S Ș N L I Ă L A Ţ T
E I S Ă S Ă G F A L R V S I I B
H C N C N Ș T D L A A H E T T L
C U I H R T D H C N E R W L E S
T A P E M E A S U R E W N Ţ Ă M
R E V I R D W E R C S F R S H Y
```

BOLT	BURGHIU
DRILL	CUI
HAMMER	ȘAIBĂ
LADDER	SCARĂ
LEVEL	ȘURUBELNIȚĂ
NAIL	ȘURUB
NUT	PIULIȚĂ
PENCIL	CHEIE FRANCEZĂ
PLIERS	CIOCAN
SAW	CREION
SCREW	NIVELĂ
SCREWDRIVER	CLEȘTE
TAPE MEASURE	SURUB
WASHER	RULETĂ DE MĂSURAT
WRENCH	FIERĂSTRĂU

Review Time: Draw lines between the English word on the left and the corresponding translation on the right. Refer back to the original puzzle if you need help.

```
G  B  H  A  L  A  T  D  E  B  A  I  E  H  E  E
S  P  A  N  T  A  L  O  N  I  S  C  U  R  Ţ  I
S  Î  E  T  Ă  K  Ă  D  F  E  X  S  C  D  U  S
Z  K  E  I  H  C  O  R  R  Ă  F  R  A  Ş  E  N
Ă  Ă  C  A  I  R  A  E  E  E  A  D  E  O  E  T
W  T  I  O  Ă  C  O  M  T  V  S  N  H  C  T  S
I  N  H  P  S  H  V  B  A  E  L  S  K  N  N  E
Ă  C  O  A  T  E  S  T  E  J  S  T  Î  Ţ  I  O
Ş  C  N  N  S  T  Ă  E  W  R  I  O  D  E  M  A
T  P  Î  T  P  L  R  S  S  E  Ş  P  Ş  Ţ  Ă  I
C  S  Ă  S  A  E  R  U  C  V  U  Ţ  Ţ  W  Ţ  G
H  Q  E  E  J  B  A  E  N  O  N  I  F  M  L  Z
I  I  T  V  A  M  S  T  K  L  Ă  P  I  A  Ă  B
P  Ş  N  O  M  S  H  H  S  U  M  Î  Ş  E  C  M
I  N  O  L  A  T  N  A  P  P  R  E  S  Ă  N  A
U  H  I  G  S  H  O  R  T  S  N  R  T  O  Î  H
```

BATHROBE	ŞOSETE
BELT	CUREA
COAT	VESTĂ
DRESS	EŞARFĂ
GLOVES	PANTALONI SCURŢI
HAT	PULOVER
NECKTIE	PANTALONI
PAJAMAS	ÎNCĂLŢĂMINTE
PANTS	HAINĂ
SCARF	ROCHIE
SHOES	CRAVATĂ
SHORTS	CHIPIU
SOCKS	MĂNUŞI
SWEATER	PIJAMA
VEST	HALAT DE BAIE

Review Jumble: The translations in the word list below have been scrambled. Draw lines between the left and right columns to find the correct translations.

```
E B L C V S N E I T U S R T E T
Î T R I K S R A T N B O W T I E
M N S Ă N Â M E D S A E C X A M
B L L N Ţ N W E D H I Ă N S B S
R O E O B A R R B N M S A W E Y
Ă G N I Ţ W R Ă I A E N R I D E
C Ţ J P E I C Ă Ş S D P Ş M M J
Ă Ă E A T O E Ă B A T R S S U A
M Â R P L Ţ L O L E E W C U T T
I O I I Î Î N S L C A O A I S Ţ
N T E S Ţ Ş Â E A Ă S V R T O T
T R N T N Ţ C L O T H I N G C C
E I A O R A K T U S B L U G I H
X H B O R C E M S U I T H Z I V
E S R B E N R J H F E H M J S Ă
Ş S A N D A L E L E T E R B Â E
```

WRIST WATCH	COSTUM
BOOTS	CIZME
BOW TIE	CĂMAŞĂ
BRA	COSTUM DE BAIE
BRACELET	ÎMBRĂCĂMINTE
CLOTHING	SUTIEN
JEANS	SANDALE
NECKLACE	LENJERIE
SANDALS	BRETELE
SHIRT	BRĂŢARĂ
SKIRT	FUSTĂ
SUIT	PAPION
SUSPENDERS	BLUGI
SWIM SUIT	CEAS DE MÂNĂ
UNDERWEAR	COLIER

Review Time: Draw lines between the English word on the left and the corresponding translation on the right. Refer back to the original puzzle if you need help.

```
S E N E T P E I P C P E P J E Ă
M P T O O Ș G O O P M A H S E D
O A Ă S P Ă H M W J O S H N M P
Ț S R P A M B A A S A S T D U E
T T A E N P A I I W U Y E E F R
S Ă T R F L H Ș H R S O K Ă R I
T D N F E C C T B S D A D R A U
F E E U A D U H O O M R O U P Ț
W D D M Ă O T L R O Ț Ș Y G H Ă
Ș I Ă E M O F A E U T R O E Ț D
N N Ț S O L N A R N J C I D R E
U Ț A T A T N C N A T O Ț Ă R D
P I H T O K C I T S P I L P A I
Ă T N A R O D O E D V A L A Z N
S E S N E L T C A T N O C E O Ț
D Ț Q U S C Ă T O R D E P Ă R I
```

COMB	SĂPUN
CONTACT LENSES	PERIUȚĂ DE DINȚI
DENTAL FLOSS	DEODORANT
DEODORANT	AȚĂ DENTARĂ
HAIR DRYER	ȘAMPON
LIPSTICK	PIEPTENE
MAKEUP	APĂ DE GURĂ
MOUTHWASH	PASTĂ DE DINȚI
PERFUME	PARFUM
RAZOR	USCĂTOR DE PĂR
SHAMPOO	RUJ
SOAP	MACHIAJ
TOOTHBRUSH	APARAT DE RAS
TOOTHPASTE	LENTILE de contact

Review Jumble: The translations in the word list below have been scrambled. Draw lines between the left and right columns to find the correct translations.

```
M U E S U M R R U Ţ X B L O Ţ T
A L A T Ş O P U I C I F O S T R
G H I Ş A E E Ă M R E F M Ş D A
A E O P O D T E O H I U N C E I
Z T U S A Ă E U G R I T A O E N
I R E I P M O P E D E I Ţ A T S
N O Z K T I O S A K I C E L E T
U P U T R O T T R R S R I Ă C A
N O M H S A S A M L T C B F I T
I R A B T T M R L A A M H G F I
V E Ă I Ş R A R V I Ş T E O F O
E A O R E F H D E R Ş I I N O N
R N A P A I J F I P E E Ţ P T L
S F U L I G H T H O U S E O S U
A S D O D R A B A R N S F A O L
L R N O B R U S T T Ă H Q N P Ă
```

AIRPORT	FERMĂ
BAR	ŞCOALĂ
BRIDGE	BAR
DEPARTMENT store	STADION
FARM	SUPERMARKET
FIRE STATION	POD
HOSPITAL	OFICIU POŞTAL
LIGHTHOUSE	MUZEU
MUSEUM	AEROPORT
OFFICE	BIROU
POST OFFICE	MAGAZIN UNIVERSAL
SCHOOL	SPITAL
STADIUM	FAR
SUPERMARKET	GARĂ
TRAIN STATION	STAŢIE DE POMPIERI

Review Time: Draw lines between the English word on the left and the corresponding translation on the right. Refer back to the original puzzle if you need help.

```
U  A  Ț  T  O  H  N  I  Z  A  G  A  M  E  R  T
C  O  A  S  H  I  G  M  Y  R  A  T  E  M  E  C
A  Q  H  P  Ă  O  A  E  Ă  D  H  N  H  A  I  U
S  A  O  A  Y  C  A  M  R  A  H  P  T  O  Ț  N
T  E  T  R  R  N  E  I  C  A  M  R  A  F  I  I
E  P  E  C  R  E  K  T  Ă  B  U  C  A  O  L  V
L  O  L  U  O  E  S  U  O  H  A  R  E  P  O  E
T  R  E  N  H  F  S  T  A  I  E  N  A  E  P  R
S  T  E  I  Y  O  F  T  A  T  L  R  C  R  E  S
A  E  R  V  S  R  T  E  A  U  K  B  O  Ă  D  I
C  A  F  E  N  E  A  E  E  U  R  B  I  K  E  T
S  T  O  R  E  Ț  H  R  L  S  R  A  N  B  I  A
A  T  H  S  E  T  N  Ț  B  A  H  A  N  O  Ț  T
R  I  T  I  M  I  C  L  H  I  B  O  N  T  C  E
N  O  I  T  A  T  S  E  C  I  L  O  P  T  E  A
H  H  F  Y  E  S  Ă  M  M  H  Z  C  D  T  S  R
```

BANK	UNIVERSITATE
CASTLE	CASTEL
CEMETARY	BIBLIOTECĂ
COFFEE SHOP	PARC
HARBOR	CIMITIR
HOTEL	BANCĂ
LIBRARY	PORT
OPERA HOUSE	OPERĂ
PARK	SECȚIE DE POLIȚIE
PHARMACY	HOTEL
POLICE STATION	MAGAZIN
RESTAURANT	RESTAURANT
STORE	FARMACIE
THEATER	TEATRU
UNIVERSITY	CAFENEA

Review Jumble: The translations in the word list below have been scrambled. Draw lines between the left and right columns to find the correct translations.

```
S M R Y L L G A S S T A T I O N
T S O O N E W A Y S T R E E T D
R N E T L O C D E P A R C A R E
A Ş E O O H R A X F F P U U T O
D U U D D R A A F S A A M C A S
Ă N T E I C C I Y R T U G U K A
C G I N E C C Y K T W T T S E B
U I Ă T E L C I C O T O M E D E
S S E C I D N A M L B M C M D N
E P N G A G I A E U E O T A B Z
N O H O L M Ş C Z N B B R F E I
S T R O I I I C C U A I A O N N
U S T E N I L O S A G L F R Z Ă
N Z D Ă D N A B N S I E F F I R
I P O T S E D R O T A C I D N I
C I F A R T R O L E Y Y C R Ă E
```

AUTOMOBILE	STRADĂ CU SENS UNIC
ACCIDENT	MOTOCICLETĂ
BUS	MAŞINĂ
GAS STATION	LOC DE PARCARE
GASOLINE	BENZINĂRIE
LANE	CAMION
MOTORCYCLE	AUTOBUZ
ONE-WAY STREET	DRUM
PARKING LOT	SEMAFOR
ROAD	INDICATOR DE STOP
STOP SIGN	BENZINĂ
TRAFFIC LIGHT	TRAFIC
TRAFFIC	ACCIDENT
TRUCK	BANDĂ

Review Time: Draw lines between the English word on the left and the corresponding translation on the right. Refer back to the original puzzle if you need help.

```
I  R  E  I  P  M  O  P  E  D  Ă  N  I  Ş  A  M
E  E  E  O  N  A  C  P  O  T  Ă  E  N  Ş  F  T
I  R  E  T  P  O  C  I  L  E  I  C  I  E  S  T
Ţ  O  E  T  P  O  L  I  C  E  C  A  R  U  R  O
I  A  A  E  R  O  G  L  I  S  O  R  B  A  E  T
L  H  O  V  E  R  C  R  A  F  T  M  I  L  B  T
O  H  I  Ă  Ă  C  T  I  E  I  A  N  C  E  A  T
P  S  S  N  Ţ  A  N  U  L  R  R  Y  I  N  V  F
E  D  U  T  O  N  A  A  I  E  C  P  C  I  I  G
D  M  B  B  S  O  A  N  L  I  H  O  L  R  O  W
Ă  L  W  M  L  E  S  L  B  U  T  D  E  A  N  I
N  T  A  E  A  O  M  E  U  O  B  T  T  M  N  Ţ
I  Y  Y  T  U  T  O  C  A  B  R  M  Ă  B  L  E
Ş  F  E  R  R  Y  D  H  D  U  M  S  A  U  T  Ş
A  U  T  O  B  U  Z  Ş  C  O  L  A  R  S  X  S
M  R  T  U  T  A  N  K  I  S  I  H  F  E  O  Z
```

AIRPLANE	BAC
AMBULANCE	CANOE
BICYCLE	TANC
BOAT	AMBULANŢĂ
CANOE	MAŞINĂ DE POLIŢIE
FERRY	METROU
FIRE TRUCK	SUBMARIN
HELICOPTER	BICICLETĂ
HOVERCRAFT	ELICOPTER
POLICE CAR	AVION
SCHOOL BUS	TREN
SUBMARINE	AEROGLISOR
SUBWAY	BARCĂ
TANK	MAŞINĂ DE POMPIERI
TRAIN	AUTOBUZ ŞCOLAR

Review Jumble: The translations in the word list below have been scrambled. Draw lines between the left and right columns to find the correct translations.

```
R O W E R B E H N F G G E C N A
H U T R U C S G E A R L N A B M
C T S I U I M M R E E E M B Ă V
N V N S N S Ă N A E E R O C C G
E B R A I C Ă C S N E G O I E E
R H P O H A Ă E O G D K B K S R
F S P O L O N E Z Ă C A Ă A E M
V I E T N A M E Z Ă R Z R N M A
G L T S P T P E D A E A F I A N
T G H A D O H M A N D A R I N Ă
F N J N L G J B O E S O A T T B
H E Ă I U I O P J F H F N A E A
E T S T S P A N I O L Ă C L I R
I H R X E J Ă N T A M O E I V A
A O E N G L E Z Ă J I R Z A O A
P O R T U G U E S E H T Ă N T V
```

ARABIC	ITALIANĂ
ENGLISH	SPANIOLĂ
FRENCH	ENGLEZĂ
GERMAN	RUSĂ
GREEK	GERMANĂ
ITALIAN	POLONEZĂ
JAPANESE	MANDARINĂ
KOREAN	JAPONEZĂ
MANDARIN	PORTUGHEZĂ
POLISH	EBRAICĂ
PORTUGUESE	VIETNAMEZĂ
RUSSIAN	ARABĂ
SPANISH	FRANCEZĂ
HEBREW	COREEANĂ
VIETNAMESE	GREACĂ

Review Time: Draw lines between the English word on the left and the corresponding translation on the right. Refer back to the original puzzle if you need help.

```
P P T O L I P I L O T I O X M O
A O O A Ț R Ă S Ă N T A P S I N
R C M L C E E Ă I N U R S E U I
O E T P I O U H T H O E T L R Ț
T W S O I Ț V S C F I S H E S P
C A I D R E I A E A I A T C A A
O A T O M T R S R R E H T T E N
D R N I N P O C T F G T R R D L
O H E E R H A R I E A O I U A
C I D N T I I I F E T H T C L W
T T T W T H A E Ă Ă E R C I G Y
O E L E C T R I C I A N A A H E
R C C Y L I G U T I N G I N E R
S T S B F T B G I Ă E Ț S G R T
E P O L I C E O F F I C E R N E
L A C I D E M T N E T S I S A E
```

ACTOR	DENTIST
ARCHITECT	INGINER
CARPENTER	PILOT
CHEF	ELECTRICIAN
DENTIST	DULGHER
DOCTOR	POMPIER
ELECTRICIAN	ACTOR
ENGINEER	ARHITECT
FIRE FIGHTER	PSIHIATRU
LAWYER	POLIȚIST
NURSE	PROFESOR
PILOT	AVOCAT
POLICE OFFICER	ASISTENT MEDICAL
PSYCHIATRIST	BUCĂTAR
TEACHER	DOCTOR

Review Jumble: The translations in the word list below have been scrambled. Draw lines between the left and right columns to find the correct translations.

```
T T H A N A I C I T I L O P H G
C T E W A C C O U N T A N T R C
S C O L R T A I L O R C Y E T A
R R M C T A H Y D O M O H S U P
E O E U I A H L S E Ă N I G L P
H I T P S D M S E C M T F U Ţ R
C T E A T I E U A T R A M Ş O O
T O F E S F C M Z A E B R T T F
U R U L O N H I A I E I A A G E
B M E R O R A Ţ A R C L P R P S
F Ă P E A R N D G N A I H E N O
R C I R E Z I R F T E P A C N R
O E O B W E C S S M E C A N I C
T L R S C I E N T I S T H A Ă I
F A Ă Ţ N I I T Ş E D M O D Y L
B R P O L I T I C I A N R C Ă A
```

ACCOUNTANT	PARAMEDIC
ARTIST	OM DE ŞTIINŢĂ
ATHLETE	DANSATOR
BARBER	CONTABIL
BUTCHER	PROFESOR
DANCER	FRIZER
FLORIST	ARTIST
MECHANIC	POLITICIAN
MUSICIAN	MĂCELAR
PARAMEDIC	INSTALATOR
PLUMBER	FLORAR
POLITICIAN	CROITOR
PROFESSOR	MECANIC
SCIENTIST	ATLET
TAILOR	MUZICIAN

Review Time: Draw lines between the English word on the left and the corresponding translation on the right. Refer back to the original puzzle if you need help.

```
M R E M R A F I S H E R M A N S
U A D S G R O A F P O Ş T A Ş E
R O I O H M O E R T C A Ă Ş Ă N
B A S L Ă T R T A M X Ă O I A O
A N N D C M S L Ă I A F V I G P
R J N I I A S I M C E C R I H B
T R U E R N R E L R U A I A M I
E A R R A E T R D A N D R S T J
N N X R N R T E I I N M A E T U
D I T I I A A E R E A R B R P T
E D I S D U L E V C R A U E T I
R Ă T N T R T I I C R D S O G E
D R E O Ă E I S S M I C S A J R
Ă G B Ş V A T V A T A D L O S O
R U G A R D E N E R E L E W E J
Z B U S D R I V E R I H S M G W
```

BARTENDER	POŞTAŞ
BUS DRIVER	ŞOFER DE AUTOBUZ
FARMER	GRĂDINAR
FISHERMAN	TAXIMETRIST
GARDENER	SOLDAT
JEWELER	JURNALIST
JOURNALIST	FARMACIST
MAIL CARRIER	BARMAN
PHARMACIST	MEDIC VETERINAR
SOLDIER	BIJUTIER
TAXI DRIVER	TRADUCĂTOR
TRANSLATOR	PESCAR
VETERINARIAN	FERMIER

Review Jumble: The translations in the word list below have been scrambled. Draw lines between the left and right columns to find the correct translations.

```
T D I O R E T S A G S C T T S M
N S I S T E M S O L A R S R A M
D Â E O T F O T O C V A S R C N
H J N C R Â O D R J H T T N V T
Y R U C R E M A U H Â E H E A M
N U T P E N T P Ă T U R N Â N E
T H P G I E I S H R I U Â E E T
E O E U R T T X A A S C Ă R A S
T G N U E H E N A E V R H Ă E Y
N E R R E L U R Â B S E R A O S
O O U A U S N E G M T M N E M R
K A T N Ă T E M O C Ă O C U O A
H Ă A U N R A M E O O P A B S L
I Ă S S L A H S U M G P L U T O
W Q N U E P Ă F T E N O I O E S
E R I N N R T G J T D A N P N O
```

SOLAR SYSTEM	SOARE
MERCURY	LUNA
VENUS	SATURN
EARTH	ASTEROID
MOON	SISTEM SOLAR
MARS	NEPTUN
JUPITER	MARTE
SATURN	CRATER
URANUS	VENUS
NEPTUNE	URANUS
PLUTO	PĂMÂNT
SUN	COMETĂ
CRATER	PLUTO
ASTEROID	MERCUR
COMET	JUPITER

Review Time: Draw lines between the English word on the left and the corresponding translation on the right. Refer back to the original puzzle if you need help.

```
N G R E N B M C T C N N T D O R
H T S A A F I U E Y V I O A R Ă
C E A T I M A L N T X E L E E H
T E R R P L L A O S R Ă Q O N T
S A X O F O N L E C N O L O I V
F H I M H T E P D I Ţ B M E R V
H L T P E F I N R I E L M B U F
H O U E E P O U O X I U I P O E
W D L T G S B N C B Z R T Ţ B N
Ă D R A E M Ă O A I M Ă Ţ S M O
M R B I A A T A C I N O M R A H
I A A T E P M U R T P U R A T P
C L O T E N Ţ N U P R A H T O O
S B W C I Ă Ţ B Ă D I S U I O X
E U E V I H A R P Ă N Ă B U T A
L L M S A C C O R D I O N G H S
```

ACCORDION	VIOARĂ
BAGPIPES	PIAN
CELLO	HARPĂ
DRUMS	CIMPOI
FLUTE	TUBĂ
GUITAR	ACORDEON
HARMONICA	MUZICUŢĂ
HARP	TOBE
PIANO	FLAUT
SAXOPHONE	CHITARĂ
TAMBOURINE	VIOLONCEL
TROMBONE	TROMPETA
TRUMPET	TAMBURINĂ
TUBA	SAXOFON
VIOLIN	TROMBON

Review Jumble: The translations in the word list below have been scrambled. Draw lines between the left and right columns to find the correct translations.

```
Z H U I R O T Ă Z E R C N Î O I
H D I A N E I W Î Â P S E T E M
N U M G Ş N Ş G W L L Ă F T Â D
O O I I L G N O I T O M E N H Ă
A R T T Y S R C O N F I D E N T
Y P P A H R T D D R W R Ţ L T A
S H F T I I Z E A S U Î T A E R
Î R S E S R S U O V R E N N O O
D N D I R U E I F Ţ A I N G A J
Â H T Ă F I R P B N Ş E E R L I
Â E Â N Ţ U C P S U O Î X Y O R
Ă Â O O F W Î I R C S C C T I G
M C M E T S I R T I A Ă I I Ţ N
D E R O B H N Ă D W S R T M Ş Î
E D E S S A R R A B M E E I H I
L E N T U Z I A S M A T D D A R
```

EMOTION	TRIST
HAPPY	CONFUZ
SAD	AGITAT
EXCITED	TIMID
BORED	FURIOS
SURPRISED	ENTUZIASMAT
SCARED	RUŞINAT
ANGRY	ÎNCREZĂTOR
CONFUSED	FERICIT
WORRIED	ÎNGRIJORAT
NERVOUS	EMOŢIE
PROUD	MÂNDRU
CONFIDENT	PLICTISIT
EMBARRASSED	UIMIT
SHY	SPERIAT

Review Time: Draw lines between the English word on the left and the corresponding translation on the right. Refer back to the original puzzle if you need help.

```
V A S C U L A R C E R E B R A L
D T Ţ H T S H A V A R I C E L Ă
I E S U T P A G L Ă K N E V Ţ L
A A E R O M I E C L P H R A A A
R Ă O I R A D M I R E I E O U Z
E K E A Ţ R E E D I A R R H E A
E A E I E C S S E I G M G G C N
U C O U G H E L U L A S P Y H E
F O U R J R T F E A B B S E I I
E L Ă U I R E U N S N E E K C G
B D L W E S B L Y I S Y S T K A
R F A V H E A D A C H E H O E R
Ă M E Z C E I N F E C T I O N O
O F C W D B D L F Ţ R S J F P M
O P A C E D E R E R U D K A O E
T R R N H I K G N E L G W H X H
```

ALLERGY	HEMORAGIE NAZALĂ
CHICKENPOX	GREAŢĂ
COLD	ECZEMĂ
COUGH	RACEALĂ
CRAMPS	VARICELĂ
DIABETES	ALERGIE
DIARRHEA	DIAREE
FEVER	CRAMPE
FLU	GRIPĂ
HEADACHE	FEBRĂ
INFECTION	TUSE
NAUSEA	INFECŢIE
NOSEBLEED	DURERE DE CAP
RASH	DIABET
STROKE	accident VASCULAR CEREBRAL

Review Jumble: The translations in the word list below have been scrambled. Draw lines between the left and right columns to find the correct translations.

```
N T G O E N N E A A C N L Y H H
N H S R H O E Ă M I G R A I N E
N C S Ă I V R Y N Ă S U R I V H
I A P E S B E F E I N B H Â A C
D M R V R R A C C I D E N T S A
H O A U I R O A O N Ţ Ă R E T H
E T I T C R T T V S T O L G M C
Â S N T N V U Ă N A E S M P I A
E E P I L E P S I E A N O O Â M
N D E M C R D E P E U L I J C O
G I W A U Â W I M U T E O A W T
E R I M T M L Y C Ă R U S R A S
A E S H Â E F R A C T U R Ă H U
U R Â T P E R U T C A R F Ă K D
T U U S N N O I S S U C N O C S
N D Y A R K C A T T A T R A E H
```

ACCIDENT	DURERI DE STOMAC
ASTHMA	COMOŢIE
BRUISE	OREION
BURN	ARSURĂ
CONCUSSION	FRACTURĂ
CUT	MIGRENĂ
EPILEPSY	ASTM
FRACTURE	VÂNĂTAIE
HEART ATTACK	INFARCT
MEASLES	ACCIDENT
MIGRAINE	ENTORSĂ
MUMPS	POJAR
SPRAIN	TĂIETURĂ
STOMACH ACHE	EPILEPSIE
VIRUS	VIRUS

Review Time: Draw lines between the English word on the left and the corresponding translation on the right. Refer back to the original puzzle if you need help.

```
C A N Y O U H E L P M E W R E I
T H L Ă T S O C T Â C O D T G R
H N Q D W O R Y U T F D A N A A
N L E D E G T N E M V H I H U T
H U W F N C L H A R W C E O R I
B S E Ţ W Â E O M I A O A Â A C
A A T Y C T C W Ă F M W H Y G T
A E U I W D U F I Ă F H O T H E
Ţ C N W O E A A N N E O Ă H L V
V E C E H D M R N M H N S A N H
Â T I S I E M I T T A H W Ă A U
H S W U C P N T H H H B Ă Ă O H
M E H A D A T U J A I Ţ O P Ă M
T T E C E R A O E D W O E T W U
F Â R E M T I E J E Â W C E R O
C C E B F E A B O O C A F O D M
```

BECAUSE
HOW
HOW ARE YOU
HOW FAR
HOW MUCH
CAN YOU HELP ME
WHAT
WHAT TIME IS IT
WHEN
WHERE
WHO
WHY

CINE
CE MAI FACI
CÂT DE DEPARTE
CE
CUM
UNDE
MĂ POŢI AJUTA
DEOARECE
CÂT COSTĂ
CÂND
DE CE
CÂT ESTE CEASUL

Review Jumble: The translations in the word list below have been scrambled. Draw lines between the left and right columns to find the correct translations.

```
M L L I B E H T V S Â A A G T E
A A E Ă N R D R I N K A F S Â T
I P S R M K E T Ş I Ş C A B Â L
N I P A O I I T E K T F I B N I
C C U E D S C O I P K R K N O S
O N Â D T E W D F A C T U R Ă T
U I N S C I P I E N W C I E M Ă
R R A Â I E Z R N J Ş G N N A D
S P I Y T I B E Â E U D E N C E
E L T U R Q D Ă R N L N M I H V
A U Â Ţ E E Q V U U Z I E D E I
C L Ă E S A E Ă N T Y T S M L N
N E O E S Ţ T C D W U Ş R T N U
Â F R T E P H S M O O R T S E R
M T A L D I T O A L E T Ă E R I
A P E R I T I V N S D F S I A I
```

APPETIZER	BACŞIŞ
BREAKFAST	CHELNER
DESSERT	MASA DE PRÂNZ
DINNER	BĂUTURĂ
DRINK	CINĂ
EAT	MENIU
LUNCH	DESERT
MAIN COURSE	MIC DEJUN
MENU	A MÂNCA
NAPKINS	ŞERVEŢELE
RESTROOMS	FACTURĂ
THE BILL	APERITIV
TIP	FELUL PRINCIPAL
WAITER	TOALETĂ
WINE LIST	LISTĂ DE VINURI

Review Time: Draw lines between the English word on the left and the corresponding translation on the right. Refer back to the original puzzle if you need help.

```
Ţ  H  S  S  R  Â  T  O  E  U  O  Ţ  B  A  Ţ  R
K  E  B  G  A  T  A  I  N  T  E  R  N  E  T  P
R  E  C  E  P  Ţ  I  E  A  R  U  E  N  S  F  Ă
S  E  I  N  T  E  R  N  E  T  L  U  T  F  C  T
D  S  P  E  J  I  Y  O  S  G  I  Ă  T  I  U  U
R  Q  E  A  H  Ţ  L  I  R  Z  S  R  N  T  N  R
N  E  G  N  P  C  D  U  I  T  O  E  O  A  C  I
S  A  C  T  T  Â  V  G  O  I  M  I  J  M  E
B  Ţ  A  E  O  I  E  D  M  G  N  A  S  N  A  H
T  A  P  N  P  L  F  L  I  M  A  C  I  A  F  L
G  O  O  Â  E  T  E  E  I  M  Y  G  V  R  P  E
Y  D  S  T  K  I  I  T  D  O  E  I  E  E  I  I
H  D  O  N  I  T  O  O  O  Ă  T  P  L  D  A  L
M  H  R  D  R  W  S  H  N  H  L  Y  E  U  S  A
O  N  P  Â  E  I  A  O  G  A  E  A  T  N  F  A
P  N  H  L  T  B  L  A  N  K  E  T  S  H  D  A
```

BED	SALĂ DE FITNESS
BLANKETS	CHEIE
DO NOT DISTURB	BAGAJE
GYM	HOTEL
HOTEL	TELEVIZIUNE
INTERNET	PAT
KEY	INTERNET
LUGGAGE	PROSOP
RECEPTION	RECEPŢIE
ROOM	NU DERANJATI
TELEVISION	PĂTURI
TOILET PAPER	HÂRTIE IGIENICĂ
TOWEL	CAMERĂ

Review Jumble: The translations in the word list below have been scrambled. Draw lines between the left and right columns to find the correct translations.

```
E H E B U S I N E S S D Y S M U
Q I I I R E C A F A F H E E G Ţ
Ţ P F E M U Z I C Ă P D D E N T
E H O A M A T E M A T I C Ă I H
C I Z L R M Ş B R O C O O D R I
N L O N I G F G I I N Ă A T E S
E O L S D M O I N O R O R N E T
I S I N J E B E M S L F C G N O
C O F F G R N I G E Z O A E I R
S P S E E E E O Ş Y D U G U G Y
C H E M I S T R Y T G I D I N O
I Y E I R E N I G N I O C A E A
S T W B O H E E A E Ş I L I C R
Y O T O T A T L I T S B N O N T
H D E I S T R A T U S N O Ţ I Ă
P E I M I H C L M F I Z I C Ă B
```

ART	LIMBI
BIOLOGY	CHIMIE
BUSINESS	MATEMATICĂ
CHEMISTRY	FIZICĂ
ECONOMICS	AFACERI
ENGINEERING	ISTORIE
GEOGRAPHY	BIOLOGIE
HISTORY	GEOGRAFIE
LANGUAGES	MUZICĂ
MATH	FILOZOFIE
MEDICINE	ARTĂ
MUSIC	ECONOMIE
PHILOSOPHY	ŞTIINŢĂ
PHYSICS	INGINERIE
SCIENCE	MEDICINĂ

Review Time: Draw lines between the English word on the left and the corresponding translation on the right. Refer back to the original puzzle if you need help.

```
X P E R P E N D I C U L A R A R
P A R A L L E L N Ă L G I R Î F
Ă N O Z A I O G F O P Î I M N R
N O I T I D D A A W I T L U M A
N I O N E V R A M T H S O L U C
V T S V O L U M E M N N I O L Ţ
R A L U C I D N E P R E P V Ţ I
E C E N D S T T O T A E C H I E
R I Y O G K I C Ă I I R Ă R R D
E L R I C C T S A Ţ T R A I E L
D P T T A D U N A R E A Ţ L A P
Ă I E C E D Ţ U E N T R U R E H
C T M A L M C Ţ I C Ă B E Q Q L
S L O R Y E O H Ţ P O A U L E Ţ
D U E F C I T E M T I R A S U V
A M G A D O T Î G Ţ I L P O L R
```

ADDITION	ADUNARE
AREA	VOLUM
ARITHMETIC	PARALEL
DIVISION	ÎNMULŢIRE
EQUATION	SCĂDERE
FRACTION	FRACŢIE
GEOMETRY	GEOMETRIE
MULTIPLICATION	ÎMPĂRŢIRE
PARALLEL	ECUAŢIE
PERCENTAGE	ARITMETIC
PERPENDICULAR	RIGLĂ
RULER	PERPENDICULAR
SUBTRACTION	PROCENT
VOLUME	ZONĂ

Review Jumble: The translations in the word list below have been scrambled. Draw lines between the left and right columns to find the correct translations.

```
T O E G A G G A B L G G L E M D
P I S T Ă D E D E C O L A R E B
O I C E A L A M A V T C N U P D
A N Z K R T Ă Y E R A L O C E D
R T P T E U I A A A T T I U E A
T E A A Ă T T R I W S V T S X I
Ă R S K Ș D W R U L N R A T T Ț
A N S E H A C E A C O U N O R I
U A P O C R P V T P E A R M O R
S Ț O F A U I O O E E S E S P Ă
S I R F S R R R R R R D T V R C
A O T R R Ă E I O T T M N H I E
Ă N S A N A T N T E R M I N A L
F A B I H G A I L Y Ț T F N D P
W L Ș E R V G I I I O J A G A B
Ș E P Y Ă I B H O Ț E Ț H F T L
```

AIRCRAFT	**BAGAJ**
AIRPORT	**AERONAVĂ**
ARRIVALS	**SOSIRI**
BAGGAGE	**INTERNAȚIONALE**
CUSTOMS	**TERMINAL**
DEPARTURES	**SECURITATE**
GATE	**DECOLARE**
INTERNATIONAL	**PUNCT VAMAL**
PASSPORT	**POARTĂ**
RUNWAY	**PLECĂRI**
SECURITY	**PAȘAPORT**
TAKEOFF	**AEROPORT**
TERMINAL	**BILET**
TICKET	**PISTĂ DE DECOLARE**

Review Time: Draw lines between the English word on the left and the corresponding translation on the right. Refer back to the original puzzle if you need help.

```
R F S L G U F T O N T U R K E Y
D N T S W P A O P F E R M I E R
H M O P H F O M S G M G U K O C
S E O P Y Ă R R N E Ţ P N E M A
Ţ Ş D A R D I E C O C O Ş Ă B T
G W C A Ă A Y K C U D L G Ă R H
K Ţ Ţ R X O Ţ A L T R A C T O R
L T K T S L L Ă A R R A G L T O
H A A D C A L U R H V C S O C O
F A M M Z M R U U P O U P C A S
T S G H E B E L B F A R M E R T
M V T S A O Ş K S W O C S R T E
Ţ B Ă E Ă A A T H O M A R E G R
A V O E E W E I E I R N Y O I Ş
T U A R L Ţ T N E K C I H C P R
B A T G T R U L P E S E Ţ E A S
```

BULL	VACĂ
CHICKEN	MĂGAR
COW	FERMIER
CROPS	MIEL
DONKEY	PUI
DUCK	TRACTOR
FARMER	RECOLTĂ
GOAT	TAUR
HORSE	RAŢĂ
LAMB	OAIE
PIG	COCOŞ
ROOSTER	CAL
SHEEP	CAPRĂ
TRACTOR	CURCAN
TURKEY	PORC

Review Jumble: The translations in the word list below have been scrambled. Draw lines between the left and right columns to find the correct translations.

```
H A T O U R I S T N Ă H O Y X H
G T S O U V E N I R S P A R C O
U Ă S B W C G N E E O U E R M L
I T N S A H A M O N U M E N T S
D R I E I Ţ A M R O F N I F I Ă
E A U D Y C U O C I S E T N H E
B E R R O R R I Ă O T T F N D I
O D R E I R E S T N R O M I F I
O E D B M N C L E S R D U A E Ţ
K I E U I A E M L M I G E I P C
V R Z U M N U V A A R R S R K A
A E R E Ţ N A T U U G L U L R R
U L R S O T I E O S H T M T A T
H A O M S O O T O F T A R A P A
Ă G S S N O I T C A R T T A I S
I G H I D T U R I S T I C E T F
```

ART GALLERY	GHID TURISTIC
ATTRACTIONS	INFORMAŢIE
CAMCORDER	VIDEOCAMERĂ
CAMERA	HARTĂ
GUIDE BOOK	MUZEU
INFORMATION	TURIST
MAP	APARAT FOTO
MONUMENTS	GALERIE DE ARTĂ
MUSEUM	GHID
PARK	RUINE
RUINS	SUVENIRURI
SOUVENIRS	ATRACŢII
TOUR GUIDE	PARC
TOURIST	MONUMENTE

Review Time: Draw lines between the English word on the left and the corresponding translation on the right. Refer back to the original puzzle if you need help.

```
O P R O T E C Ţ I E S O L A R Ă
C R D L O P A T Ă J A L P O Ă S
H D S O H O S A N D C A S T L E
E G U R S S T W B S S F A E I V
L D R A U G E F I L H E R R A A
A R F M N N L S T M L A Ă U A W
R Ă I A S T D D S Ă M L N B S W
I E N V C A E Î G A Ă I T Î D O
D J G L R H N K T P L B N D O B
E N H A E A I I C I Î G E G R N
S R T S E Î S R S U Ă A N O E G
O H A C N D I O U I B C C U A D
A Ă O O I Ă P E J L P E R I S W
R M T V S I W A H C A E B H E U
E T O U E B Y S A N D V V L E I
S X N A H L Ţ I A Ă A E N E O V
```

BEACH	ÎNOT
BUCKET	MARE
HAT	PĂLĂRIE
LIFE GUARD	NISIP
OCEAN	GĂLEATĂ
SAND	OCHELARI DE SOARE
SANDCASTLE	SALVAMAR
SEA	SOARE
SHOVEL	OCEAN
SUN	LOPATĂ
SUNGLASSES	VALURI
SUNSCREEN	CASTEL DE NISIP
SURFING	PLAJĂ
SWIMMING	SURF
WAVES	PROTECŢIE SOLARĂ

Review Jumble: The translations in the word list below have been scrambled. Draw lines between the left and right columns to find the correct translations.

```
V R E F F W A W R A O Y G A L C
M N U Î B A R C T R X N H Y A H
Q D J S H A E D A Î Y B D J R S
T T N M D L G E A R E S M F D T
X O H F L N J O P L D S Ă O Î H
Ă D Ă U S O N I G Ă A Y F J Î L
E A B O R A H T N J E M R A G G
O U P T Ă Z S U P Î S B A D D H
E P S H N N T A N N A S T E W E
D B E C I T A Ă Ă G U H C M G Î
C M T L A N Î E M G I B E U Î Î
P H T L U T S D B C R R E L N E
I M L O Ă E R O R I A A L A G D
N S T W R A R O F M O A L E U I
O E I V H H I G H T M T Y Î S W
T C W O R R A N Î S C Ă Z U T T
```

BIG	SCUND
SMALL	SCĂZUT
WIDE	MOALE
NARROW	USCAT
TALL	GREU
SHORT	LARG
HIGH	BUN
LOW	MIC
GOOD	ÎNALT
BAD	RĂU
WET	ÎNALT
DRY	MARE
HARD	ÎNGUST
SOFT	UMED

Review Time: Draw lines between the English word on the left and the corresponding translation on the right. Refer back to the original puzzle if you need help.

```
K P L A D L N T Ş H M A U Ş D G
A E V I S N E P X E L W P D O F
U L V E N O P A E H C T T A Î A
A E E W A I T H Î N Î L A C S A
E Î X S O P Ş O O H T G U U R E
Î R Ş Î A L P T M T N R Î O Ş O
G I D E I R S Q I O A M T E N F
D I R T Y A M Ş R T G H R H Î P
U D F U F D E W A H N Z T N N S
S N N Y O R D T T A S R C R E W
E G I E G U E C E R S E L A G Y
Î G N T J M S L I Ş T I B P S S
D E E Ş F I C O U S H N H I C H
U L P E A E H S Q Ş G Ş O D U T
S E O A N F I E R B I N T E M R
H Î N C H I S D N I R E C E P B
```

FAST	GREŞIT
SLOW	RECE
RIGHT	CURAT
WRONG	ÎNCHIS
CLEAN	SCUMP
DIRTY	IEFTIN
QUIET	DESCHIS
NOISY	ÎNCET
EXPENSIVE	FIERBINTE
CHEAP	ZGOMOTOS
HOT	DREAPTA
COLD	RAPID
OPEN	LINIŞTIT
CLOSED	MURDAR

Review Jumble: The translations in the word list below have been scrambled. Draw lines between the left and right columns to find the correct translations.

```
T  B  I  A  Ş  D  M  G  N  I  N  N  I  G  E  B
A  P  T  P  Â  E  M  P  T  Y  T  O  I  Î  E  T
F  U  L  L  D  S  L  F  F  S  E  T  O  L  Î  R
S  T  U  P  E  C  N  Î  Ş  A  V  Ş  L  O  P  U
E  E  E  W  N  H  R  I  I  E  Ş  E  Â  I  Ş  I
G  R  E  Ş  S  I  T  O  C  Y  A  W  H  G  G  D
L  N  I  A  L  S  H  H  E  Y  Ş  T  T  Â  O  Z
Ţ  I  O  Ţ  A  G  I  T  T  G  H  I  L  E  Ţ  R
T  C  G  R  B  E  L  H  E  G  H  U  Ţ  Ţ  I  O
I  W  O  H  T  U  T  N  C  S  O  H  S  M  B  B
W  Ş  L  Y  T  S  S  J  W  N  Î  H  F  U  D  H
U  U  B  J  U  E  W  N  U  E  Î  S  Â  A  T  Â
H  Ţ  T  E  P  D  T  T  N  D  A  H  R  O  E  E
G  E  U  L  V  Î  E  D  Ţ  R  S  K  Ş  O  L  N
B  V  Ş  J  U  R  H  P  G  L  I  C  I  F  I  D
R  A  Ş  H  D  I  F  F  I  C  U  L  T  A  S  Y
```

FULL	VECHI
EMPTY	NOU
NEW	UŞOR
OLD	GOL
LIGHT	ÎNCHIS
DARK	SLAB
EASY	DIFICIL
DIFFICULT	ÎNCEPUT
STRONG	GRAS
WEAK	DESCHIS
FAT	PUTERNIC
THIN	SUBŢIRE
BEGINNING	SFÂRŞIT
END	PLIN

Review Time: Draw lines between the English word on the left and the corresponding translation on the right. Refer back to the original puzzle if you need help.

```
T Â R Z I U R T N U Ă N Î Î W H
T D Ă O A A L H A O Â A P H Ă Î
H D E C E U B T E D U I R L B N
T C O N M O W I S R Â T N Î M A
U L T I M U L W D H E E S N N I
O Ă R A F A A H T E L T O I A N
H P Â A T I S F Î E V S F R D T
T U W E C I T W Ă A P R O A P E
I D S I I C I T S R I F E A D D
W F I C O H Z O A L Ă D T M B E
N D U M X C L F P Y I T I T E P
A D E M U Î W H Q S O I H Ă F A
Z K Ă K V S G E N T Î U D E O R
D O T E E O V I E S Â I H S R T
S H Â R E M Ă N I Ă T B T H E E
U Î I C A N E Y S M G Î I N Y O
```

NEAR	DUPĂ
FAR	TÂRZIU
HERE	DEPARTE
THERE	APROAPE
WITH	ACOLO
WITHOUT	DEVREME
BEFORE	AFARĂ
AFTER	AICI
EARLY	ULTIMUL
LATE	PRIMUL
INSIDE	CU
OUTSIDE	FĂRĂ
FIRST	ÎNAINTE DE
LAST	ÎNĂUNTRU

Review Jumble: The translations in the word list below have been scrambled. Draw lines between the left and right columns to find the correct translations.

```
R D S P L A T I N U M E T A L T
N V B C U A I Ţ R L Ţ A C A N C
D O T E T L O P N D H N Ă F M U
I A Ţ O G V U W B G R Ţ N N A E
T N Z E O C O E A R B M P C T Ă
V Ă S E L O T U L Ţ S I L V E R
T H Ă Ă D O Ţ D A N M A A S R T
T F I O N I L I T Ţ Y V S P I A
O U M S C I A A R G I N T L A I
D H W O S N T M A T E R I A L P
I R Y I L D E A O E A C C S U B
X A A E O G M N L N O I E T I R
T D M Ă L C I T S P D N O I G P
D N T A R E R H P O O R O C Ă A
T A S T E E L E E T E R C N O C
R S U F A Y R V S W A A M V L U
```

CLAY	CUPRU
CONCRETE	STICLĂ
COPPER	MATERIAL
DIAMOND	OŢEL
GLASS	DIAMANT
GOLD	PLASTIC
MATERIAL	LUT
METAL	LEMN
PLASTIC	AUR
PLATINUM	METAL
SAND	PLATINĂ
SILVER	PIATRĂ
STEEL	NISIP
STONE	BETON
WOOD	ARGINT

Review Time: Draw lines between the English word on the left and the corresponding translation on the right. Refer back to the original puzzle if you need help.

```
V U L I B A D I X O N I L E Ţ O
I Ţ I L P H E L A T O F I E R L
L S O Â E E T E L Q W S T O E E
Ă H S C I M E N T N C U T A B E
E C U C P I E L E A O T T R B T
Ă Â A L A M Ă S U M E H A H U S
Â Y L B I E P C M B E S W N R S
E C S E M Â I L E R S C Ă O X S
T E I I A U H R U N W O E T C E
F T Ă T C D B I E M O L L T Ă L
L R J R H E N Â K P B R T O R N
T H O Â U I R C E R A M I C Ă I
S A E H M M I A A S W P T L M A
Ă S S U T R R M M U I N A T I T
E H L T B M B A Â I M Ţ N F D S
I A L U M I N U M H C R H Ţ Ă U
```

ALUMINUM	TITAN
BRASS	HÂRTIE
BRICK	CĂRĂMIDĂ
CEMENT	SOL
CERAMIC	PIELE
COTTON	CIMENT
IRON	FIER
LEAD	BUMBAC
LEATHER	PLUMB
MARBLE	CERAMICĂ
PAPER	OŢEL INOXIDABIL
RUBBER	MARMURĂ
SOIL	CAUCIUC
STAINLESS STEEL	ALAMĂ
TITANIUM	ALUMINIU

Review Jumble: The translations in the word list below have been scrambled. Draw lines between the left and right columns to find the correct translations.

```
T Ă A C F T A I W H S S Ş W S Ş
E N G A P M A H C T Ş L Ş D E D
T U S N O E I N A P M A Ş N A C
R G T R C T V Ş P H K J Ş F E O
W Ş K R E R E B Y D E C U S F A
R H L W H A I B O A M S T I A Ă
W H I S K Y Ă V F I N N H P C Ă
R N M S L T L O D C I H I E A E
E B O S K T Y D S U O O F P P R
T E Z Ă F E L C C R Ş N Ă H P B
A E E Q O U Y Ă T U E O I E U L
W R A F M O B D W M E D R A C A
D A W D F Z G I N Ş Ş G W N C N
H O E S T O E T P A L A L I I I
C A P P U C C I N O R H D G N V
H I L A C E Y A I R H B H V O E
```

BEER	CONIAC
BRANDY	WHISKY
CAPPUCCINO	BERE
CHAMPAGNE	VIN ROŞU
COFFEE	CEAI
GIN	LAPTE
JUICE	ŞAMPANIE
MILK	CAFEA
RED WINE	SUC
RUM	ROM
TEA	CAPPUCCINO
VODKA	APĂ
WATER	GIN
WHISKEY	VODCĂ
WHITE WINE	VIN ALB

SOLUTIONS

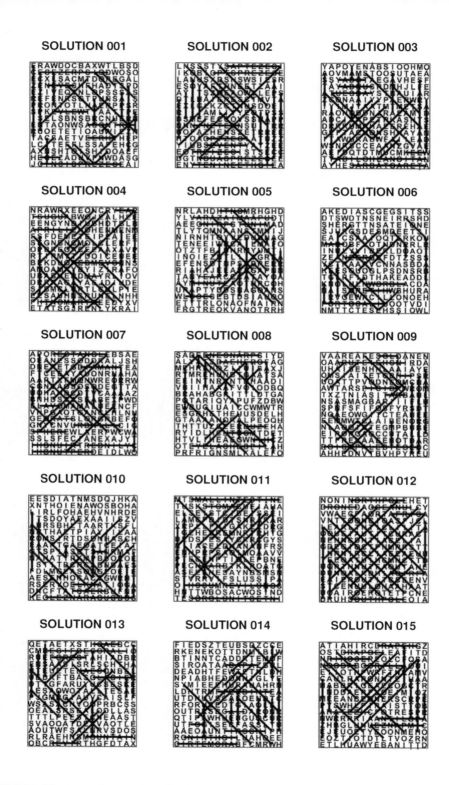

SOLUTION 001 SOLUTION 002 SOLUTION 003

SOLUTION 004 SOLUTION 005 SOLUTION 006

SOLUTION 007 SOLUTION 008 SOLUTION 009

SOLUTION 010 SOLUTION 011 SOLUTION 012

SOLUTION 013 SOLUTION 014 SOLUTION 015

SOLUTION 016

SOLUTION 017

SOLUTION 018

SOLUTION 019

SOLUTION 020

SOLUTION 021

SOLUTION 022

SOLUTION 023

SOLUTION 024

SOLUTION 025

SOLUTION 026

SOLUTION 027

SOLUTION 028

SOLUTION 029

SOLUTION 030

SOLUTION 031

SOLUTION 032

SOLUTION 033

SOLUTION 034

SOLUTION 035

SOLUTION 036

SOLUTION 037

SOLUTION 038

SOLUTION 039

SOLUTION 040

SOLUTION 041

SOLUTION 042

SOLUTION 043

SOLUTION 044

SOLUTION 045

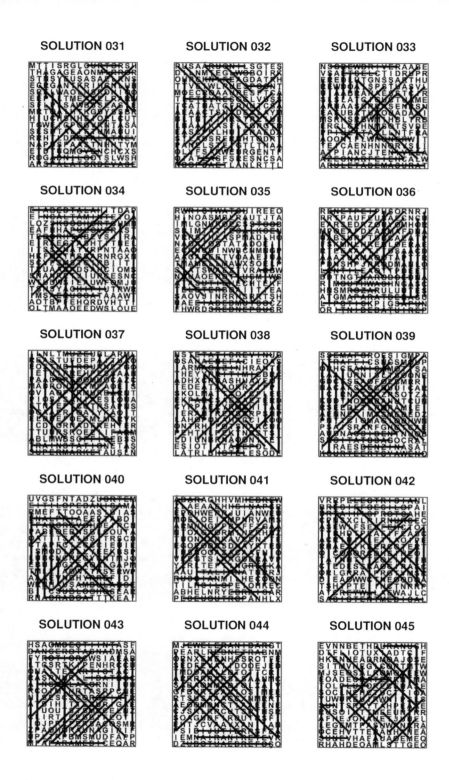

SOLUTION 046

SOLUTION 047

SOLUTION 048

SOLUTION 049

SOLUTION 050

SOLUTION 051

SOLUTION 052

SOLUTION 053

SOLUTION 054

SOLUTION 055

SOLUTION 056

SOLUTION 057

SOLUTION 058

SOLUTION 059

SOLUTION 060

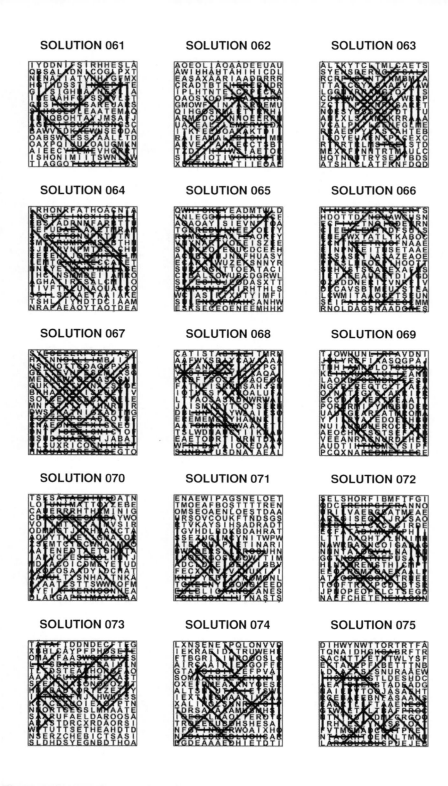

SOLUTION 061

SOLUTION 062

SOLUTION 063

SOLUTION 064

SOLUTION 065

SOLUTION 066

SOLUTION 067

SOLUTION 068

SOLUTION 069

SOLUTION 070

SOLUTION 071

SOLUTION 072

SOLUTION 073

SOLUTION 074

SOLUTION 075

SOLUTION 076

SOLUTION 077

SOLUTION 078

SOLUTION 079

SOLUTION 080

SOLUTION 081

SOLUTION 082

SOLUTION 083

SOLUTION 084

SOLUTION 085

SOLUTION 086

SOLUTION 087

SOLUTION 088

SOLUTION 089

SOLUTION 090

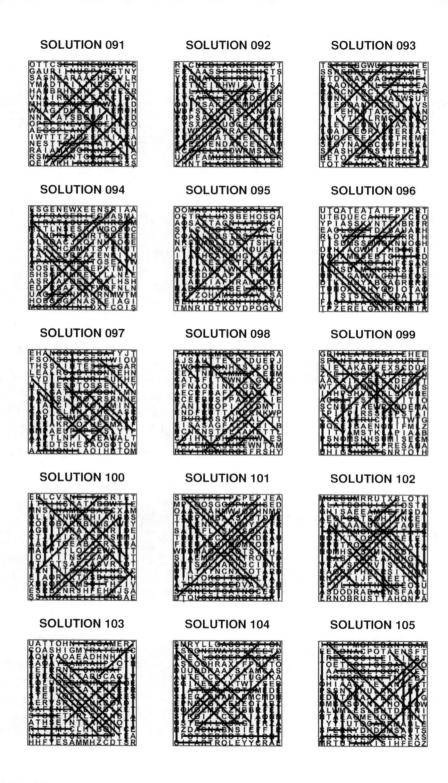

SOLUTION 091

SOLUTION 092

SOLUTION 093

SOLUTION 094

SOLUTION 095

SOLUTION 096

SOLUTION 097

SOLUTION 098

SOLUTION 099

SOLUTION 100

SOLUTION 101

SOLUTION 102

SOLUTION 103

SOLUTION 104

SOLUTION 105

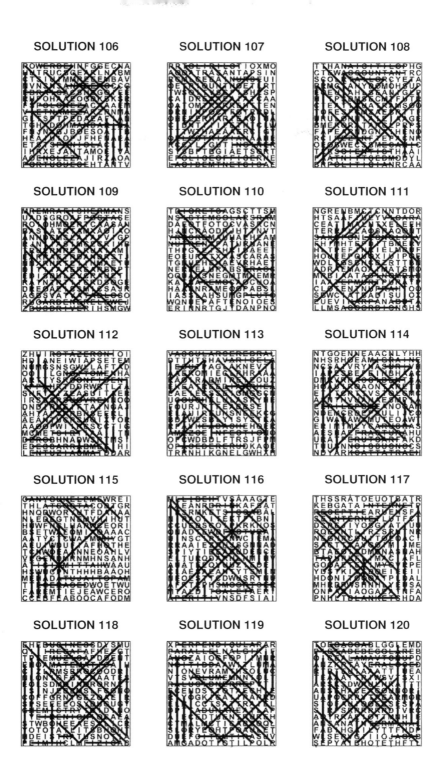

SOLUTION 106

SOLUTION 107

SOLUTION 108

SOLUTION 109

SOLUTION 110

SOLUTION 111

SOLUTION 112

SOLUTION 113

SOLUTION 114

SOLUTION 115

SOLUTION 116

SOLUTION 117

SOLUTION 118

SOLUTION 119

SOLUTION 120

SOLUTION 121

SOLUTION 122

SOLUTION 123

SOLUTION 124

SOLUTION 125

SOLUTION 126

SOLUTION 127

SOLUTION 128

SOLUTION 129

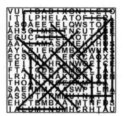

SOLUTION 130

Wordsearch Books by David Solenky

Language Series
Learn French with Wordsearch Puzzles
Learn German with Wordsearch Puzzles
Learn Hungarian with Wordsearch Puzzles
Learn Italian with Wordsearch Puzzles
Learn Polish with Wordsearch Puzzles
Learn Portuguese with Wordsearch Puzzles
Learn Romanian with Wordsearch Puzzles
Learn Spanish with Wordsearch Puzzles
Learn Swedish with Wordsearch Puzzles
Learn Turkish with Wordsearch Puzzles

Baby Name Series
Baby Name Wordsearch Puzzles
Baby Boy Name Wordsearch Puzzles
Baby Girl Name Wordsearch Puzzles

Made in the USA
Middletown, DE
18 March 2019